Wanderings:
A Pilgrim's Walk on This Good Earth

Greg DeLoach

Parson's Porch Books

Wanderings: A Pilgrim's Walk on This Good Earth
ISBN: Softcover 978-1-949888-37-9
Copyright © 2017 by Greg DeLoach

All rights reserved. No part of this book may be reproduced or transmitted in any form or by any means, electronic or mechanical, including photocopying, recording, or by any information storage and retrieval system, without permission in writing from the publisher.

To order additional copies of this book, contact:

Parson's Porch Books

1-423-475-7308

www.parsonsporch.com

Parson's Porch Books is an imprint of **Parson's Porch & Book Publishers** in Cleveland, Tennessee, which has double focus. We focus on the needs of creative writers who need a professional publisher to get their work to market, **&** we also focus on the needs of others by sharing our profits with those who struggle in poverty to meet their basic needs of food, clothing, shelter and safety.

To Amy, my beloved, and my sons Clark and Aaron, who inspire me to walk gratefully.

Table of Contents

Preface 9

Part One: Blazing Trails

Pilgrim's Walk 13
Meaningful Work 15
Don't I Know You? 17
I Smell a Bear 19
I See a Bear! 21
Benedictions and Invocations 23
Bored to Death 25
Beginning (or continuing) the Journey 27
Belonging Around a Campfire…and to One Another 29
Baking and Breaking 31
The Beloved Belonging 33
Turn the Page 35
Yom Kippur for the Rest of Us 37
Please, Walk on the Grass… 39
Keeper of Bees 40
#justlove 42
In Search of Our "Laughing Place" 44
Don't Take Baby Jesus 46
An Uncertain Life 48
A Brand-New Lunch Box 50
Broken Down and Rusted Out 52
A Forty Dollar Tomato?! 54

Part Two: The Long Trek

Have you ever heard a stone speak?..59
Dirty Pickup Trucks and Jesus..61
Burial Ground of the Stars..63
Better Boys Among Us...65
A Little Walt Whitman is Good for the Soul …......................................67
Fragments of a Life..69
What Does God Look Like?...71
Walking Across the Street One Sunday..73
Pork Skins and Diet Coke...76
Our Place in this World...78
Not-so-pleasant Surprises..80
Muffin Top Drop..82
In-Between Addresses...84
Enough..86
Does Your Well Hold Water?..88
Baptizing Kevin...89
Am I My Brother's Keeper?...91
An Inconvenient Truth..93
A Spare or a Prayer..95
A Selfish Article..97

Part Three: Journey of Gratitude

A Life of Gratitude 101
Friends.. 103
A Lamp unto My Desk... 105
Seeing and Saying Thanks 107

I Am "Running" Out of Shoes 109
Daddy Joe 111
Whatever Happened to Generation X? 113
Send Me a Text… 115
What is Church? 117
Our Shabby Biographies 120
Recall Notice 122
Living Up to the Smile 124
Old Notebooks 126
Hugging Trees and Thanking God 128
If There Was One Word… 130
Broken Things… 132
Going Places 134
Seeing the World Through My Dog's Nose 135

Part Four: Wandering with Mystery

A Place to Call Home 139
Disabling an Omnipotent God 141
Bro is No Mo 143
Dark Energy 145
Time is… 147
When the Earth Falls Away 149
Silence Can be Deafening 151
The Last First 153
Peace for the World – And All Therein 155
Life and Death are Not So Far Apart 158
For Everything There is a Season 160

Faded Pictures and Faded Memories 162

Before I Die… 165

Blood Moon 167

All of Life Summed Up in a Cashew Can 169

Losing in Order to Gain.. 171

A Wandering Life.. 174

A Generous Stack of Wood 176

You Are Not Your Own 178

The Grace of Doing Nothing 180

Preface

This is a book of reflections on wandering. It could be said that if you stick to a trail you are less likely to wander, but even on a trail one can happily wander. The only trails I knew about growing up were the ones worn deep by the dairy cows sauntering across the pasture. In spite of having acres of broad pastures to meander across, cows inevitably take the same singular path leading them to and from the dairy barn. In fact, if a cow ever wandered off the beaten path, so to speak, it most always meant something was wrong.

As a child, the cow paths seemed onerous and restrictive. But I have come to love a good trail, especially when I am making my way up or around a mountain. There is comfort in a trail, because it is a reminder that others have gone before you. Most trails are marked by a blaze, usually a symbol painted on the side of a tree or the face of a rock. On the Appalachian Trail, there is a blaze every 8th mile of a 2" x 6" rectangle, painted in reflective white. Even though much of the AT is a rather defined and clear path stretching from Georgia to Maine, there is still the need to be reminded that this is the right trail.

Cairns are another way to mark a trail. It's basically just a big pile of rocks. Sometimes they mark an intersection; and other times they mark a new beginning or ending. Often times, like a well-worn path, it is simply a reminder that others have gone before you. This is not unlike the ancient altars that were erected in the times of Abraham, Isaac, and Jacob.

There is a wonderful story in the Hebrew Scriptures of Samuel setting up a stone and naming it Ebenezer, saying "Thus far the LORD has helped us." (1 Samuel 7:12) This image is its own kind of ancient blaze reaching across generations of pilgrims.

When I see a blaze on a trail, or a pile of rocks piled up into a cairn, I am reminded of the faithfulness of the trailblazers that have gone before me. There is also the assurance of an ancient presence; a host or great cloud of witnesses doing their part to encourage me to stay on the path.

We all are traversing this good earth, which means we are given the opportunity to not only make a mark, but as importantly, encourage one another navigating through the terrain called life. There are sacred texts, ancient liturgy, and contemporary stories to guide along the journey.

This collection of writings is a simple attempt to share my own marks and experiences along the way as well as an invitation to meander alongside my own thoughts, musings, and reflections. Like trails, some of the pieces will take you places with a specific destination or point. Others are winding walkabouts where I am just thinking out loud to no one in particular.

The stories themselves are not connected, other than the threads of grace weaving throughout. And while they are organized along four main sections, they can be read in any order the reader likes, or in no particular order at all.

I hope you enjoy Wanderings and I hope you have someone to share your stories of faith, doubt, and pilgrimage on this good earth.

Part One: Blazing Trails

"The Mountains are calling, and I must go…"
                                                John Muir

Pilgrim's Walk

When we walk it is usually to just get from one place to another. I am accused by friends and family that I walk "too fast," and I suppose that is true. I tend to charge ahead with a fixed destination in mind. I am the same way about hiking in the mountains. Whether shouldering a backpack, or just simply going out for a daylong trek, I march forward as if I am in a race. I guess I like the strain and the push, and deep down I am competing against something – but I will let others psychoanalyze it.

There are other times we walk when the point is not so much the destination, but the walk itself. The word "meander" comes to mind. Strolling is another lovely and quaint way to phrase walking for no particular point other than the pleasure of it. Walking is a great way to clear your head or work through a problem. Some walk for exercise with a determined gait and others walk leisurely with a friend for companionship.

Aristotle allegedly taught his students while strolling about. Sigmund Freud conducted consultations while walking and directed a number of "walking analyses" in the evening times. If Steve Jobs wanted to have a serious conversation with you, his preference was to do it while walking. Harry Truman was a man who loved routine and one of those daily routines was a vigorous walk of a mile or two at 5 AM – wearing a business suit and tie.

One of my favorite gifts is a walking stick one of my sons whittled for me from a young dogwood. In the last 15 or so years that stick has travelled with me along the mountain ridges of North Georgia, North Carolina and Tennessee. I am guessing I have hiked easily over a thousand miles with that walking stick. Every time I pick it up I think of my family and give thanks and then launch into a hike down a trail.

In the Gospels, many things happened while Jesus was on the road with his disciples – healing, teaching, praying, feeding, and listening. One of the most beloved post-resurrection stories is his walk on the road to Emmaus.

Discipleship is best described as a journey – "a long obedience in the same direction," as Eugene Peterson phrases it. During the Christian Year we are reminded of these "sacred walks" through Advent and Lent, but I also find the long season called "Ordinary Time" equally compelling. Sometimes the walk is not an easy one, as with Holy Week culminating in Good Friday. Sometimes the walk is neither good nor bad, just, well, ordinary. Like life itself, there are moments where we lose vision and focus and doubts will obscure the way. The walk, however, is not a solitary journey, but one made in community. We need each other, now more than ever, in worship, in community, in fellowship, and in discipleship.

We are all on a pilgrim's walk following a path where others have gone before. May your walk, your journey, your hike, and your meander be a time of personal and corporate growth in love for others and for this world that God loves so much.

As Jesus was walking along…he said…"Follow me." (Matthew 9:9)

Grateful to be on this trek with you…

Meaningful Work

I count it a grace that most of my life has been filled with meaningful work to do. I am grateful for health that allows me to sweat over tilling a garden, or splitting a pile of firewood, or sprinting down a corridor in a hospital to visit a loved one. I am grateful for a mind still sharp enough (but not that sharp) to articulate a thought into action and a dream into a plan.

Work that means something is meaningful work whether it is repairing a car, stitching up a patient, or cleaning a house, or helping feed a friend.

In my teens, I remember many days standing on the wet, concrete floor of the dairy barn looking out to the pastures as the morning sun began to warm the sky with color and light. I gazed longingly and hopefully for something more.

Growing up on a dairy farm there was always work to do, and to be candid, I rarely appreciated it. Everyone knows that cows have to be milked twice a day, every day, but there are so many other chores. There were endless miles of barbwire fences that needed to be repaired or replaced, leaving hands and arms nicked and bleeding. My shoulders still ache with the memory of digging holes for fence posts. Cows not only needed to be fenced in, they sometimes needed to be found. When a cow gave birth, it is not uncommon for the cow and calf to go into hiding in the woods. This seemed to happen a lot on Friday evenings, just as my brothers and I were planning to go out on the town. Instead cruising with our friends, we wandered out into the woods until we could find the missing members of the herd. Each year barns had to be painted, manure had to be shoveled, hay had to be bailed, and pastures had to be cut.

Most of my growing up years was spent gazing beyond the barn looking longingly and hopefully for something more.

Reflecting back through those many decades I am learning that the "more" that I was searching for was right "there." I am not romanticizing farm life, nor am I regretting subsequent decisions that led me off the farm. Rather I am acknowledging that all we have is now, just now.

Meaningful work is not reserved for the poets or preachers. It is approaching each task as a sacred moment, an opportunity to experience and thereby express higher notions than just "getting the job done."

There are days, many days than I care to admit, that I worry a bit about what kind of work I will do in the future. Will I ever be able to retire? Will I even want to retire? Will others want me to work with them; for them? I don't have answers to such questions.

I just have now. And I have work to do. And I am thankful that in some small way I get to participate in the holy vocation of life through work.

My favorite poet and essayist, Wendell Berry, wrote the following poem titled, "The Real Work."

It may be that when we no longer know what to do
we have come to our real work,
and that when we no longer know which way to go
we have come to our real journey.
The mind that is not baffled is not employed.
The impeded stream is the one that sings.

Don't I Know You?

Through the years I have attended my share of banquets. When you are a minister, you get invited to a lot of them and nearly as often you are invited to sit at the head table and offer a blessing, a welcome, or a benediction. One such banquet I was involved in a rather innocent exchange with a gentleman seated to my right. His name was Dr. Clarence Williams. We were seated at the head table because I was invited to give greetings on behalf of the religious community and Dr. Williams was invited to give greetings on behalf of the medical community. Between mouthfuls of food – I never let conversation interfere with eating – he asked me where I was from. I shrugged and said, "Eatonton; you probably never heard of it." He then went on to say, that yes, in fact, he did know it quite well. "I taught at the High School for a few years before I went to the Medical College. My wife is from Eatonton. In fact, I know some Deloaches." I proceeded to name the DeLoaches in my family and he shook his head and said, "I only remember Greg DeLoach; is he any kin?" "Well that's me," I blurted out.

It turns out he taught at my high school while I was a student. I never had him for a class, but he said he remembered me attending a class next door. I wondered, and still do, what in the world did I do, say, or how did I behave that would cause him to remember me thirty years later. As I ponder this, I am not sure I want to know the answer. Suffice it to say I was touched that he reached across three decades to connect with me.

Just a few days after that particular banquet I was part of another large gathering for a meal - Wednesday night dinner at church. As I typically do, I was wandering from table to table speaking to church members and stopped by to chat with Sophia, age four. She gave me a big hug and a bigger smile and asked, "Did you see me last week?" I honestly could not remember, but instead of engaging her in a nuanced dialogue around the limits of middle-age memory, I said, "You know, I think I did." She responded with great delight,

"Noooo…. I wasn't here!" Howls of laughter from parents and grandparents filled the fellowship hall. Zinged by a four-year-old!

Sometimes I will casually greet someone only to be asked, "Did you miss me? I have been out of town travelling." I feel like I have been set up. "I have been sick, so you have probably wondered where I have been" or something like that, but I am thinking, "I cannot keep up with everyone, all the time." Still, I work up a concerned smile, give them a hug, and say, "Well, I am glad you are here today."

To be noticed…deep down we all want to know we matter to someone else. While out of shyness, modesty or just simple introversion there are some who want to be as inconspicuous as possible, I think everyone wants to matter to someone else.

Jesus noticed a solitary widow offering meager coins to a Temple treasury when others were busy with the wealth of others; he saw little children coming to be blessed when others saw distractions needing to be shooed away; he saw a woman stooped with infirmity when others only saw a breach in protocol.

One of the great missions of the church is to see: to see injustice; to see brokenness; to see loneliness; to see pain; to see joy; to see opportunity; to see others. In church, we gather to pay attention to each other and to all others and take notice. It is a call to look *in* the eyes of Jesus and see the freedom that awaits because we do not have to be captive anymore. It is also a call to see *with* the eyes of Jesus those who are bound and fettered, lost and lonely, the least and the last, and set them free.

And when we see with the eyes of Jesus, or when we are seen by Jesus, the darkest powers no longer have a hold anymore.

"Don't I know you?" is a holy claim and a sacred commission.

I Smell a Bear

Since our boys were infants, Amy and I would take time at least once a year to take them camping in the Great Smoky Mountain National Park. Every year held a new adventure: poison ivy from the firewood; an unexpected rain coming through an unexpected hole in the tent; ants in the s'mores; and of course, bears.

One year I was out hiking by myself on one of the back-country trails. The views are always glorious and the trail is nearly always peaceful. I am armed with a walking stick, some water and a pocket knife. A cell phone is not much good on such long hikes since there is no coverage, but I carry one anyway just in case there is a need to identify the body.

Around mile five of the hike I began to smell the distinct odor of a wet dog and in my mind, I thought, "Oh great, there is a bear in the vicinity." The odor would not go away and so I developed a mental plan of action of what I was to do if I met a bear on the trail while so far away. I decided my first plan was to turn around and head back to camp. Still, the smell of the wet dog followed me and so I imagined the bear had identified me as a possible snack. Granted, there are only 70 deaths caused by black bears since 1900, but I did not want to be 71.

As I picked up my pace hiking back to camp and pondering my mortality as well as my escape plan, I mindlessly readjusted my hat. It seemed every time I raised my arm to readjust my hat I would once again detect that wet dog smell. Finally, it dawned on me that the smell of the wet dog was not a bear, but me! In fact, after a few days of camping without a bath or shower there was a good chance the bears of the Great Smoky Mountains were actually avoiding me.

That is camping for you – one adventure after another. One of the many things I like about camping is the mobility. All you need is a tent (and you don't really need that most days) and a good map (which I usually ignore – it's a man thing). Most everything else you need to enjoy a few days in the woods should fit right on your back. Mobility and flexibility is the key to happy camping.

Not a bad metaphor for the faith. A faith *on the move*…going places. It is too bad so many are content with just staying put in their faith journey - never changing, never growing, never blossoming into anything more. Like water, such a faith is in mortal danger of stagnation. Water that is not allowed a place to flow becomes putrid and useless. That is why so many refer to faith as a journey or pilgrimage. As a people of God, we each lean across the next horizon for the opportunity, the next possibility.

Break camp and move on; a people on the move and God who is out there in front.

I See a Bear!

One year my beloved wife had decided she had enough of my solo hikes in the woods and decided it was time she and the boys joined me for a day hike. I picked out a nice 6.2-mile loop hike. I knew the trail well: two miles following a fast-moving creek, followed by another couple of mile up and around a mountain, interspersed with gaps and ridges that allowed for gorgeous views of the range of mountains in the Smokies. Around mile three things were not going so well as a family. Mountain trails are by their very nature, well, mountainous. Amy was getting tired, and I failed to pack water. By mile four some in my party were wondering if the trail ever went downhill. While I may sound a bit paranoid, I am certain there were times on that hike that she looked at me as if I designed the mountains that way on purpose.

It was at this point in the hike that I leaned over to my youngest son and said that in a few minutes we would reach the top and then begin a rapid decent back to camp. I told him that I was planning to move ahead "double time" and fetch some water for their mother. Just as I had shared with him my plan, I heard a bumbling commotion of snapping branches and tumbling rocks. Before my mind could fully comprehend the sound a blur of black fur rushed by me. I turned around to my wife and eldest son and said in a voice of urgency "catch up with me, there is a bear." About that time my son was staring at the face of the bear and my wife passed all three of us on the way back to camp.

A little motivation goes a long way!

The stock market fluctuations (sometimes described as a "bear market") can motivate some to spend less and save more. An illness in a family can motivate loved ones to put aside petty divisions and spend more time together. A death can motivate one to take inventory of their life.

Jesus motivated a woman caught in the act of adultery by forgiveness. He motivated fishermen hungering for something bigger in their lives to go and change lives. Jesus motivated through stories, through miracles, through presence and most of all through the good news of God's love.

What motivates you each day? How does the kingdom of Heaven, the new order of God, motivate you to change your life and work to change the world?

John Muir once quipped: "The mountains are calling and I must go." For others the bears are moving and I must get out! For all of us, life, like a winding, open trail, beckons us forward. What will you do, as poet Mary Oliver writes, with your one wild and precious life?

Benedictions and Invocations

Those words usually come in the reverse order – invocations and benedictions. An invocation is a prayer offered at the beginning of something where we are asking that our hearts may be full and open to receive the presence of God in this particular gathering. In simple, earthy terms, it is a way of saying "Good morning God!" Benedictions come at the end and they are blessings spoken over our departing. "Go with God."

When we moved our eldest son into his college dorm room, and a couple of years later did the same thing for our youngest son, I thought of the prayers of benedictions and invocations. Though they went to different colleges – one up in the north Georgia mountains, and the other in flat, pine-topped South Georgia – both move-ins were hot and muggy. It really does not take that long to move in a freshman. There are relatively few possessions to have to transport since most dorms – these days they are actually called residence halls – come more or less furnished. In some ways we, and all the other parents milling about, are the ones dragging the chore out. It is apparent after just a couple of hours that it is time to go. Friends arrive as we are about to leave, and we overhear plans being made for the evening and weekend before the inevitable first class on Monday morning. After a quick hug and kiss we shared the ubiquitous parting many parents give on similar occasions. I remember it went something like, "We are proud of you…have fun…but not too much fun…if you need us call us…here's a little spending money…be careful…remember that we love you."

Driving away felt like a benediction, a blessing over the new journey of college and career, and our new journey as empty-nesters. And yet it was an invocation too. We are saying goodbye to one part of our life and hello to another. In both benedictions and invocations, we need the blessings as we depart into the new journey as well as the assurance that God goes with us into the waiting future.

We practice this as liturgy because we live this in life: benedictions and invocations; invocations and benedictions. Sometimes a minister speaks it; sometimes a friend shares it; sometimes a family member lives it. It is a genuinely good life to have those moments and embrace them as they are claiming God's presence or pleading for God's guidance.

Sweet and sacred is the life when we are able to mark these beginnings and endings with prayers of presence and blessing. I remain grateful to share a bit of this journey with so many I call friends, family, and fellow sojourners of faith.

Bored to Death

I admit that I have unrealistic expectations of my preaching. Anytime I catch a parishioner nodding off during one of my many salient points, I feel a bit, well, incredulous. And then I delude myself with excuses for the sleepy church members, assuming, for example, that perhaps they are on medication, or working through the night on a marble sculpture, or providing security details for our government. Surely, they are not…*bored!*

At least no one has died from my preaching, like the young man in Acts 20:7-12. This episode takes place in a lighted (and presumably warm) room, late in the evening and Paul the apostle is speaking. He talks, and talks and talks – for four hours he speaks. Over in the corner, sitting in an open window is a young man named Eutychus. His name means well-fated, but he did not think so at the time. I wonder if his parents made him come to church that night?

Eutychus fell asleep – one of those deep sleeps – and fell right out of the window, down three stories. Some sermons, it seems, will kill you. It turns out Eutychus lives up to his name, because Paul grabs him by the hand and just like that Eutychus is alive and well and Paul goes back to preaching all night long!

To my knowledge I have never killed anybody with my preaching, but truthfully over the years I have seen my fair share of Bible-believing Christians get a solid nap in while I am preaching. I remember during one evening service, when my boys were still in elementary school, one of them fell into a deep, deep sleep. His rest was more or less going unnoticed until he started to snore…loudly. At that point, I knew I had lost the attention of the congregation and it was time to call for the hymn of commitment and call it a night. Unlike Paul, I know when to say when.

Young man Eutychus is literally bored to death, but is resurrected. He will not stay on the margins, to be forgotten about sitting on a window sill. The church has always depended and needed those on the sidelines to not only keep us authentic and relevant, but to give us new life and vitality.

God is about resurrecting and giving new life to sinners and saints;
    to youth and children;
        to elders at home alone and
            to singles bored and disengaged
                to church-goers and church-haters;
                      to the God-fearers and the God-doubters…

…I cannot help but believe that the resurrection means something not just in our history books but to humankind today and to the next generation who inherits it all; to take the saving, resurrecting power of Jesus and press forward.

Christ trusts all this over to you. Will we just sit here, bored to death, or will we rise up and go? Does church matter? You bet your life it does.

Beginning (or continuing) the Journey

How do you begin a journey? Do you have to have all the details worked out before making that first step or do you just tromp ahead and let the surprises be the point? Amy is a planner and loves to make (and strictly abide by) lists. I, on the other hand, tend to just plunge ahead, impulsive and at times foolish.

One New Year's Eve Amy and I "tromped" into the New Year, so to speak, by hiking five miles through nearly a foot of snow near the Amicalola Falls in North Georgia. As a reward for our modest efforts, we spent a cozy night at the Len Foote Hike Inn. You can only access this inn by hiking in and hiking out. Perhaps the term "inn" is a bit generous. It is rustic, bare-bones, and no-frills. They do provide a hot meal at night and one more in the morning before sending us back out into the snow to hike back down the mountain. It was a lovely way to close out the year and prepare for the start of a new year.

In this particular jaunt, Amy depended on me for the details since I do most of the hiking and backpacking. Wanting to make a good impression, I worked a bit harder on some of the details and she, likewise, trusted me with some of the surprises. Fortunately, our surprises were mostly positive and even when things were less pleasant than planned (like frigid temperatures in our bunk room) we made plans to adjust (I brought a winter sleeping bag that was warm and toasty).

Each new day and each new year is in itself a journey. I admit that is a worn-out analogy, but nevertheless true. And as we hike out into the start of any given day, we confess that we are all just beginners. Each waking moment we carry out halting steps into paths – some well-traveled and others quite new. Sometimes we are prepared and other times we are completely surprised, even lost.

While I often like the solitude of a good hike, where I can get lost, so to speak, in my thoughts and pace, it is always a fine thing to have a traveling companion. Indeed, at the heart of our shared humanity is the confession that we need one another – the community of faith – because we are making this trek together.

Belonging Around a Campfire…and to One Another

Whenever we can find a way to stretch out a weekend, Amy and I will slip away for a few days of camping in the Smoky Mountains. She calls it her happy place. It is mine too. A favorite time to go is in the middle of fall when leaves are in their full autumnal glory and the mountains glow with color. We love the mountains even though we did not grow up in the mountains. Neither did our parents or their parents or their parents. We both hail from Middle Georgia environs surrounded by gentle, rolling hills where the closest thing to a mountain was the fire ant mounds. Yet each time we lose ourselves "up there in the hills" and huddle around a campfire we feel a certain reconnection with our past. Many of Amy's best childhood memories are of family camping trips. My grandparents rarely left the dairy, but the two or so times I remember them traveling it was to head to the mountains. One time it included taking my brothers, sister and me to see those mountains for the first time.

Every time we are up in mountain territory – in a tent, on a trail, a hotel room, or just riding along the winding highway – we feel a reconnection, a belonging as if we have always been there.

Deep within every one of us is the need to belong. Young children take pride in belonging to their parents; adolescents carve out new identities and belong to their friends; emerging into adulthood there is the need to belong to independent ideas and convictions; and it is not uncommon that as we grow older in our adulthood we seek out our past recovering what and who we are and to whom we belong.

What a lovely place a congregation can be as pilgrims gather together, seeking to reconnect with the past as well as face the unknown future. Whether one is a crusty, old, established church member going back many generations, or simply a straggler passing briefly through, all want and seek the same thing: to belong.

Each time in such sacred gatherings we are cultivating a time of belonging in Christ. Like a drive in the mountains where an old homesickness is stirred up, we are at our best when we can sense a hunger to connect; to belong. This happens in what is ceremonially called worship. Hymns or praise music; sermons or testimonies; high liturgy or simply casual – worship can be a beautiful dance with one another and the Most High God.

Cultivating a time of belonging happens around the table too – and here I mean the supper table. Wednesday evening meals; covered dish suppers; or pot-luck lunches are some of my favorite times of belonging. Walking among the tables and speaking – even if it is briefly – to children doing their homework while rushing through a meal; catching up with harried adults who are moving quickly between work and home; and seniors who come early to see their friends are some of my favorite interactions as a minister. Belonging.

The biblical and liturgical image is the table that Christ has set inviting us to come, sit, and share. Belonging is God's gift to us and our gift to one another. This is church. This is belonging.

Baking and Breaking...

...bread, of course. For most of us bread is both abundant and taken for granted. Except for the annual threat of a snowstorm which rarely manifests, grocery store shelves are filled with bread in more choices than we can name.

Store bought bread, however, tastes...store bought. That is why I prefer baking my own bread or finding a local baker to purchase a loaf or two. Baking bread can be both fun and frustrating. Like most anything homemade, the ingredients are important, and not just what goes in, but how much, how long, etc. One of the things I appreciate about making and baking bread is that the mixing and kneading is done largely by hand. Observing the dough's feel and texture is important, because something as little as humidity can alter the outcome.

Once bread is all mixed and kneaded you leave it alone and wait for the yeast to do its work. It may take an hour, or two, but slowly and steady the dough rises and the loaf takes shape. It is then ready for the hot oven and soon the kitchen is full of the yeasty smell of fresh bread! (don't you wish this book was scratch and sniff? Go ahead, lean into the page – you know you want to!)

The best part of fresh baked bread is not in the making or the baking, but the breaking. Even better, is when you can break bread with people you love. Many Saturday evenings, if we do not have other commitments, Amy and I (and sometimes my boys when on the rare occasion they are home) will sit in our back yard and share fresh bread alongside olive oil for dipping. We also enjoy baking bread to share with friends and neighbors.

Baking and breaking - a beautiful movement of life in God.

There is so much dumped, added and mixed into our lives - good and bad and indifferent – that exceeds our control or understanding.

We live our years mixing it all together, kneaded and being kneaded, shaped and formed by the very hand of God. And then come those times when nothing seems to be happening; stillness and quiet, solitude and perhaps a bit of loneliness. Like yeast in dough, however, these can be our most formative moments, when our true shape is being revealed. Then the ovens! The trials, the testing, and the enduring.

Easy analogies in the writing, but we are well aware that living is no waltz across the dance floor. How is God shaping you? How is God shaping your family; your community?

Furthermore, how do we see our life and our mission being shared? Like bread divided among people you love, so it is with our very lives. Life is best when shared. It cannot, in the end, be hoarded away thinking that we live for ourselves alone. Our sharing is not merely among those we love, but even, perhaps especially, among those we don't – our enemies, those different from us, the strangers, the poor.

Through the ages the poor and the least of these are disdained and disregarded for not having enough bread; for not working hard enough; and so on.

Imagine living up to the vision of Christ: the city on a hill that cannot be hidden! God has made something wonderful in each life and our wonder is best and fully realized when we share it with others. No wonder Jesus compared the Kingdom of God to yeast mixed in flour – abundance comes in the sharing.

Blessed is the life that is shared among others.

The Beloved Belonging

Beloved. What a powerful word. It means that you and I are chosen of God. Our faith teaches us this in Genesis 1:26 - *So God created humankind in his image, in the image of God he created them; male and female he created them.* The Latin phrase sums it up in the beautiful phrase *Imago Dei*, Image of God.

Belong. I have written earlier about the need to belong.

Belonging happens in churches where it does not matter who you are or what you know or where you come from. What matters is that you are welcome.

Belonging happens when a kind word is shared with a stranger while patiently (or as often impatiently) waiting in shopping line.

Belonging happens with smiles, hugs, and tender touches.

Belonging happens around the tables of homes where a simple meal, lovingly prepared, is blessed and shared.

Perhaps that is the central mission of God: to invite us into beloved belonging; to be reminded of the sacred inheritance that we each reflect God's image; to know, really know, that we are loved of God and hold value to our Maker. The stories of the sufferings of Christ and his death and burial are stories not to alienate us, but connect us and remind us that even in suffering and death, nothing will "separate us from the love of God in Christ Jesus our Lord." (Romans 8:39)

When you know that you are beloved you know that you belong. Every human being was created by God as beloved in order to belong.

I hope you find your belonging. And when you do, make certain that you allow others to belong too.

"...Our humanity comes to its fullest bloom in giving. We become beautiful people when we give whatever we can give: a smile, a handshake, a kiss, an embrace, a word of love, a present, a part of our life...all of our life."

— Henri J.M. Nouwen, *Life of the Beloved: Spiritual Living in a Secular World*

Blessed to belong as God's beloved.

Turn the Page

This particular year began homeless. Well, not really. We are making due with a few worldly goods stuffed in a couple of suitcases while staying with some dear friends (who are, thankfully, still dear friends). The house we lovingly called home for ten years in Augusta was sold and turned over to new occupants. We moved to the Atlanta area on New Year's Eve, but did not yet have a place to call home.

Not only was I homeless, I was unemployed. Well, that is not quite true either. I was soon to start a new work and ministry, but at the start of the year I felt a bit unmoored. For the first time in 28 years I did not have a sermon to write, let alone a church that wanted to hear from me. And although I projected confidence to my new colleagues at my new job, I knew, and they did too, that I did not have a clue what was going on. For my first month in this New Year at the agency I honestly felt like I was just making it all up until I could figure it out.

Each day, especially in the early days of that fateful year, was the turning of another heavy page in the book of life. Everything was new, different, and at times a bit overwhelming. But soon we moved into our "new" house – built in 1985 – and placed familiar furnishings that helped transform the house into a home. Soon I was invited to speak at churches for Sunday mornings, Sunday evenings, and Wednesday nights. Soon I was learning not only the names of my co-workers, but more about the "business" of our ministry and with each passing day I was gaining authenticity in my projected confidence.

The summer before this "Big Year" my family and I were on vacation with a couple of other families. This is an annual ritual we have shared for well over a decade. We love those folks and cherish their friendship. On the beach, watching the waves roll in and the surf roll out, I was sharing with one of our friends, Monica, about the anticipated year of changes we were facing and confessing my own emerging grief with the inevitable goodbyes and wondering about what the future was going to hold with all my unanswered questions. She gently said, "Just turn the page."

She was right. Just turn the page. Which is what we all do, but rarely think about when life is normal, predictable and comfortable.

So, my wife and I have been turning pages that year, which, truth be told, we have been doing all of our lives anyway. Throughout our many decades of loving each other we have rarely known what to expect with each turning. We have moved six times, raised two boys, grieved the passing of family members, said hello and then good-bye to churches I have pastored, and on and on the pages and chapters turn and still turn.

John Lennon's song "Beautiful Boy" has a sober line, "Life is what happens while you are busy making other plans."

As each passing day comes to its inevitable conclusion, and the new morning is still on the horizon, let us live today, fully, completely, and authentically. Each day we turn a page and read with wonder and expectation of the rest of the story that is still being written.

"[Jesus] set his face to go…" (Luke 9:51)

"…but this one thing I do: forgetting what lies behind and straining forward to what lies ahead…" (Philippians 3:13)

Yom Kippur for the Rest of Us

I have never been one to stay up for the arrival of the New Year, mainly because staying up that late is difficult for me. I am an early riser by nature and nurture, which means staying up much past dark is a chore. For fifty years now I have discovered that the New Year arrives whether I am awake or not. Still, I like the days leading up to the New Year as well as the days following it, because it affords me a time of reflection. This secular holiday is a type of religious experience for me.

Each year, usually in the early fall, my Jewish friends observe Yom Kippur, which is a kind of New Year. It marks the end of the year and a time to prepare for the coming year. Yom Kippur, meaning "Day of Atonement," is the holiest day of the year for Jews around the world. I admit the name itself sounds a bit foreboding and heavy.

In contrast, New Year's Day is pretty much a secular day around the world, prefaced by parties and over-indulgence. For me it serves as my own kind of Yom Kippur. It provides me the opportunity to look back, reflect, ask forgiveness and see what I need to do for the coming year that will be different, better, and more compassionate.

Only a fool thinks one can live life without regrets. Life for all of us, honestly reflected upon, always has regrets. We look back and see failures, disappointments, and lapses of judgment, and wrong turns - most of which cannot be undone. Like the prodigal son, on some level we all squander a bit of the life that God has given us. And so, in looking back we acknowledge before God our frailty and dependence.

The practice of confession and repentance are essential for Jews and Christians alike. We take inventory to learn; to engage hope; and to re-imagine life in the New Year.

Atonement, like Yom Kippur, is essential too. Atonement literally means to be made one (at-one-ment) with God.

And I believe beyond all of the other theological divisions that are often drawn up, the one thing that can unite us and give us strength is the idea, the belief, that God wants to be made one with us. Anything else leaves us divided, partial, and fragmented.

The fragmented remains of last year are just a memory. For me there is so much good that I gratefully encountered. There are a few missteps, mistakes and disappointments too. Thus far God has brought me and I look ahead trusting that God will see me safely into another year, one day, one moment, at a time.

Shalom y'all.

Please, Walk on the Grass…

We are accustomed to reading negative signs these days. They usually begin with "No" and then detail what it is, exactly, you are forbidden to do. Signs like, "No Parking", "No Swimming", "No Fishing", "No Spitting", "No Kidding" come to mind. Perhaps you have entered a restaurant and read the sign: "No Shoes, No Shirt, No Service" (of course you would never read such a sign in any respectable BBQ stand). I have had a few ideas for some negative signs. There should be a sign declaring a "No Whining" zone, buffered by a "No Complaining" perimeter. How about a "No Surly Attitudes" for some of you who have homes populated by, well, surly attitudes? I have always felt like a "No Excuses" sign might help keep things running smoothly.

When I was a student in seminary we had a beautiful campus green right in the center. There were signs posted all around the perimeter: "Please, Walk on the Grass, But Don't Make Paths." Now that is a sign I can live with. Not only is it positive, but it's pretty good theology.

By God's good design we have been created and invited to travel through this life enjoying God's provisions. A path, however, is an imprint that scars not only lawns, but communicates to all those who follow "My way is THE way." The truth of the matter is only Jesus can make that claim: "I am the way, the truth and the life" (John 14:6). Anytime we feel as though we have the corner market on how things are done we are traveling perilously close to idolatry - we are making paths, scarring lawns, and discouraging others from doing anything different.

Church is an invitation to follow God's Way (not Greg DeLoach's, or anybody else for that matter). So please, come, walk on the grass, but don't make paths. That is a sign I can live with!

Keeper of Bees

There was a time in my life when I was no friend of a bee. Bees sting and bees can hurt. I am not allergic to bees, but I am allergic to pain. In spite of my past history with bees, there was a brief season, due to the generosity of a thoughtful church member, I was a keeper of bees. It turned out to be a glorious experiment that, unfortunately, ended with what apiary experts call "a collapsed colony." It happens. Looks like the bees were no friend of mine after all.

During that particular summer of beekeeping I would walk out each morning to the hive to wish them a good day and every evening I would lean in close to the entrance of their home and wish them a good night. I wanted to name them, but there was right at 20,000 of them and it was challenging to tell them all apart. Plus, they fly so fast. I never thought insects that sting would bring me such pleasure, but they most certainly did. Now whenever I see a honeybee flitting about a patch of clover or darting in and out of a flower, I smile and I am grateful for these wonderful insects.

I am amazed that such a tiny insect – about a half of an inch – can be so wondrously designed. One queen controls the entire colony. Now that is power. The workers carry on the vital task of pollination, gently filling the hive with pollen, nectar, wax comb and honey. They even talk with each other in a coded dance telling where to find the next great patch of pollen: "past the poplar, left at the geranium, and there you will find a large bed of lantana. Watch out for the creepy guy with a beard. He always wants to stop and talk to you. Ignore him." What amazes me is that the bees know to come back home at the end of each day. They know where they belong and how they belong – each with a function and purpose. Wondrous stuff, don't you think?

The most enduring image of the church is not far from this hive that perched in my backyard: a place to belong. Churches have changed dramatically over the centuries. Theology, liturgy, architecture and polity are as diverse as the languages of the nations. And yet all churches need to be places where connections are made and belonging is experienced. Otherwise a church is just another institution on the edge of irrelevancy.

Churches will always be making changes because that is how you survive. Just like a hive that needs to have its frames replaced or a location change, life moves forward in a flow of change that is life-giving. One thing, however, must never change. Churches must be a place and a people that no matter how far one has traveled, one can always come home and find a place. Through dedication of babies, baptisms of young believers, and tender hugs from aging seniors, church is the one place where no matter who you are, and where you have come from, Christ waits at the door with arms open wide saying, "Welcome home."

Love is God's radical vision for humanity. A church may be pardoned if the paint is peeling or the music is staid, or the sermon is dull, but it cannot survive long without a mutuality of trust grounded in unconditional love. Let's keep on being the church that God envisions.

Grateful for my place in this ecclesiastical hive.

#justlove

I suppose Valentine's Day is as good as any day to market love. One year if there was a prize I could give, I would have awarded it to McDonalds for its marketing of love. For the month of February random customers were selected to pay for their items by simple expressions of love: a fist pump to the staff…call your mom and say I love you…give a customer a hug…tweet a friend - #justlove. McDonalds called it "Pay With Lovin" campaign. I am not much for fast food, but I really like their approach. It is quirky, simple, playful, and needed.

From football to politics we are jaded with skepticism. Polarization over ideas and partisan ideology has created a culture of eroding civility. What we need is love, plain and simple. I congratulate all those who sense a need, a hunger, to love and be loved and have responded with welcome marketing efforts.

Love, true love, cannot be completely marketed – not by a company and not with a holiday. Love can only be given away. My friend David Hull, who is a coordinator for the Center for Healthy Churches, writes that churches ought to be the place where love is expected and shared. In a newsletter, he states: *A church might ask the following questions of herself related to "marketing love:"*

- *Will people recognize us as followers of Jesus by the way we relate to one another? "I give you a new commandment, that you love one another. Just as I have loved you, you also should love one another. By this everyone will know that you are my disciples, if you have love for one another." John 13:34-35, NRSV*
- *If we do love one another as Jesus loved us, do we limit that love to those who are like us in our own circle of church friends, or are we willing to share this love with people who may be very different from us but who hunger for love?*
- *What will we do as a church to "market love" by freely giving it away?*

I have no beef with McDonald's on their campaign (did you catch the pun?). It is a great idea for them to market love for February. For those of us who call on the name of Jesus as Savior and friend, love is not seasonable, marketable, or an alternative. It is just love.

May they know we are Christians by our love, in season and out.

In Search of Our "Laughing Place…

In my hometown, we still remember a man who grew up on a plantation on the east side of the county (just a couple of miles from my family's dairy). As a boy, he listened to the enslaved Africans tell folk stories that originated in West Africa and beyond. When he grew up, Joel Chandler Harris brought those stories of Brer Rabbit, Brer Bear and Brer Fox to life through print. Not many people today know much about the "Tales of Uncle Remus," but those stories were a steady part of my own upbringing. We read them at home and at school.

Our town is so proud of these beloved tales that there is even a statue of Brer Rabbit at the court house square in "downtown" Eatonton. About five years ago a few young men thought it would be funny to steal the statue. This turned out not to be funny at all because in the dismantling of the rabbit, an ear broke off and an Eatonton "APB" was issued. The assailants panicked, ditched the rabbit in the woods, but eventually confessed to their bunny burglary. The statue of Brer Rabbit has reassumed its prominent place on its podium in my dear town.

One story of Brer Rabbit is about his "Laughing Place." Space does not allow the sharing of the whole story, but one line is sufficient: "Everybody needs a laughing place."

Lord knows, *everybody needs a laughing place*. Where is your laughing place? Growing up our kitchen table was the source of our family's laughter as stories were told (and retold), as well as the usual teasing and antics that are part of a big family. While we shared jokes, most of our laughter came from stories of family members long since departed. All these years later when my brothers and sister and our families get together at the home place, our "briar patch" becomes a laughing place.

Everybody needs a laughing place. There is plenty of sadness and tragedy that deserve our somber attention. But even in this flawed and marred creation, the voice of God radiates through smiles and mirth. James Weldon Johnson poetically retells the creation story with the lines: "Then God smiled, And the light broke…" (*God's Trombones*)

The church is a wonderful spot to claim as a laughing place. We are more than the collection of the frozen chosen. We are God's people, created out of God's good pleasure with the mandate to fill the earth with our presence, our stewardship and (my translation/interpretation) laughter. It does my heart good to look out every Sunday and find occasions to share a smile, a snicker, and a laugh. I think it does God's heart good too. Leonard Sweet writes: "God's time is dance time…'Party times' are those intelligent celebrations in life when one wholly enjoys existence, when one fully plays in the theological universe. *Play* and *pray* do more than rhyme." (from *Soul Salsa*)

Enjoy your utterly unique and significant life God has given you. Share your laughter with others, and find a place this Sunday to call your "laughing place."

Don't Take Baby Jesus

Every town and city has something that caters to the tourist. In my little hometown, you can take a brief (and I mean brief) tour of the Uncle Remus Museum and purchase some sweet, Brer Rabbit swag. Over Augusta for one special week thousands upon thousands gobble up anything marked by "The Masters Tournament."

Recently I was in the city of San Antonio for a small conference. During a break, I walked down to the Alamo to do some site seeing as well as look for trinkets to bring back home. In one shop filled with gaudy and goofy souvenirs there was a display of nativity sets, with the following sign:

Don't take baby Jesus
Please, it is a set. Thank You

Apparently pilfering baby Jesus is a problem near the Alamo. Thinking about this some more, there is a deeper truth than just defending a shopkeeper's merchandise. If you take Jesus, you have to take everyone that comes with Jesus.

In a culture we are used to customizing nearly all things towards our personal taste and nearly everything can be reduced to a commodity. Jesus, however, comes as is and along with Jesus comes a family of people that many would rather leave out. Reading the Gospels Jesus brought along Samaritans and Canaanites who were ethnically and religiously on the "wrong side of the tracks." He associated with despised tax collectors, prostitutes, and other unsavory characters. Jesus reached across the cultural divide and gave women hope, the diseased healing, and the neglected life. Because of this Jesus offended those who wanted to leave all these others out of the family of God. If you take Jesus, you have to take everyone that comes with Jesus.

I did not buy the nativity set because, well, I do not need another one. I do wish, however, the sign was for sale. It would make for a nice banner across the pulpit and above the doors of the church to remind everyone that if you take Jesus, you have to take everyone that comes with him. Yes, it will inevitably offend. It will also eternally bless, and that is a gift that cannot be bought in any shop or store.

There is no need to make a banner or wear a t-shirt, button or hat with this sign. What you and I can do is take the message into this waiting world to those who want so badly to belong.

I am grateful that somewhere along the way someone invited me in to the family surrounding Jesus where I knew I belonged with all the other characters.

An Uncertain Life

In the midst of my 50th year of walking this good earth, I was wandering through a period of deep transition. Through what seemed to be a long period of prayerful discernment, accompanied by many miles of evening walks with my wife who patiently listened to me talk out my thoughts, fears and hopes, I walked away from one part of my journey and embarked upon something entirely new. The change would involve us relocating. At about the time of year when homes in our neighborhood were being decorated for the fall, our home of ten years was put on the market; quickly sold, and we were scrambling to pack our things away to live in temporary quarters. As others were packing away Christmas decorations, we were once again zipping up suitcases and moving away from church I pastored for over ten years, as well as our young adult sons living elsewhere in the community, to start a new life and work.

For about a month we moved in with some dear friends while we waited to close on our next house. We thoroughly enjoyed their company and the rekindling of old friendships, and cherished revisiting familiar places. Still, it was a time of change; uncertainty.

It is indeed an uncertain life. And so, it is for all of us, even those convinced that what they have and what they know is fixed and immovable. We are all dwelling between certainty and uncertainty. Each day is its own new year filled with new possibilities. Just today I read a delightful quote by Charles Kettering: "My interest is in the future because I am going to spend the rest of my life there."

Yes, this grand yet mysterious future is always before us where little is certain. All we can do is move forward into the certainty of loving and being loved. Where some preach fear and retaliation in the face of uncertainty, I will join my voices with the chorus of others whose purpose is to live out the commands of the Hebrew Scriptures: Love God…love your neighbor. Jesus said all the other commandments rest on these two.

My first Sunday after our move I visited a church. As I sat in worship I was loved in the liturgy of the people expressing love for God. I admit I squirmed a bit when it was time for the sermon because for so many Sundays that has been my time to share words of love. But this Sunday I was loved by the words of others.

For the benediction, the minister proclaimed the words of Henri Frederic Amiel (1821-1881):

> Life is short, and we do not have much time to gladden the hearts of those who make the journey with us. So... be swift to love, and make haste to be kind. And the blessing of God, who made us, who loves us, and who travels with us be with you now and forever.

Grateful to share this uncertain life with you, to love and be loved!

A Brand-New Lunch Box

Remember that feeling of butterflies in the stomach when you started preparing for all the things you would need for school? As a first grader, I joined the ranks of other six-year-old boys and girls across America outfitted with a book satchel, jumbo pencil, a set of crayons and a brand-new lunch box. I still have that lunch box and thermos sitting on my bookshelf at home and nearly every time look I at it I feel the faint butterflies of long ago wing their way up.

When school is in session we see them – children with their lunch boxes at the ready, boarding school buses with backpacks bulging with new notebooks, highlighters, pens, pencils and scissors. Some kids are so loaded down they look as though they are preparing to summit Mt. Everest. Some of those very backpacks are also filled with some anxiety.

Is there a time or place in your life that you would like to "go back"? Youth? College? Newlywed? Empty-nester? Yesterday? Nostalgia is the sweet recollection of the past aided by rose-colored hindsight. All we can do in going back to our past is to draw on our memories. Beyond that, God has created us to be a people moving forward.

Just like a kindergartener boarding the school bus for the first time, we often face the future with a mixture of excitement and dread. But we must step forward. We have no way of knowing what is before us: the future for our families, our health, our careers, and church are all hidden in the mystery of God. In Ecclesiastes 3:11 we read that God "…*has made everything suitable for its time; moreover, he has put a sense of past and future into their minds, yet they cannot find out what God has done from the beginning to the end.*"

We are created and destined to lean forward into the future and to do so with trust. Blessed is the one that has others to share in the journey forward. In the meantime, and this really is the only time that counts, let's enjoy today and offer a prayer of thanks for every child we see boarding a school bus.

Broken Down and Rusted Out

Out hiking on a trail, I have encountered a few surprises over the years. Deer, snakes, skunks and elk live in the woods, so I do not know why I should be surprised whenever I see them in their home. Bear also call the mountains home, so from time to time we have to share a trail.

Recently, I was out hiking with a friend (if you are going to encounter a bear it is good to have a friend, preferably one who is slower than you). We were deep in conversation when we rounded a wooded corner, and there to the side of the trail was a beat-up, rusted out old car. Trees were growing around it, indicating it had been there for quite a few years. In fact, outside of the narrow walking trail, there was no other sign of a road. It was as if the heavens opened and placed this old car alongside the trail. I suppose someone decades ago ran out of gas, or maybe had a flat, or simply blew the motor, and simply parked it.

Broken down, rusted out, and discarded. This happens to people too. Someone ceases to be useful and gets "parked" or discarded or forgotten. It happens to the elderly, to the disabled, to the meek, to the terminated. It happens when you are the wrong race, gender, political persuasion, or _____ [fill in the blank].

The truth is we are all broken in places. Some things you see: a wheelchair, a cane, a cast, a Band-Aid – symbols of broken bodies. Some things, perhaps most things, you do not see because they are buried deep beneath the effortful facades and barriers that come by way of suppression and shame. Only the bearers of such brokenness see, but even then, it can be too confusing, too overwhelming, to really see, let alone understand.

There is a lovely Latin phrase that reminds us that even in our broken places, we bear God's image. The *Imago Dei* is the understanding that all persons are gifted as bearers of the image of God. No one image is whole or complete or definitive. We need each other and not because we are whole, or perfect, or useful. We need each other because we each reflect God's image, even in our brokenness.

You and I are God's handiwork and we are "…fearfully and wonderfully made." (Psalm 139:14) In Psalm 8 we hear the prayer, "…what are human beings that you are mindful of them, mortals that you care for them? Yet you have made them a little lower than God, and crowned them with glory and honor." (vv 4-5)

Sometimes all we can see in others (and ourselves) is the brokenness, like a beat-up old car in the middle of nowhere. Lent is the season to remember that it was Jesus who took up fragmented bread and fed the multitudes and later said to his disciples "remember me" when you eat this broken bread.

What is it in your life and those around you that is less than whole, broken down and rusted out? Ernest Hemmingway wrote: "The world breaks everyone, and afterward, many are strong in the broken places."

There is no junk in the kingdom of God. Just people like you and like me. Blessed is the one who stumbles among the wreckage and sees the beauty.

A Forty Dollar Tomato?!

One of the rewards of gardening is growing and eating your own food. There are few things that can compare with sitting down at the table and knowing that the peppers garnishing the peas and the slices of tomatoes alongside the bowl of spinach all were planted, nurtured and harvested out of the garden in the back yard. Of course, my two little plots do not have much room for little else than tomatoes, peppers and a few varieties of herbs. Still, there are few things better tasting than a homegrown tomato. Can I get an amen?!

I figured my tomatoes averaged about forty dollars apiece, which does not include my labor in planting, staking, tending, watering, fertilizing and chasing away pests like hornworms, squirrels and other varmints. I certainly did not garden to save money. Someone once reminded me that it was still cheaper than paying a therapist, which I concede is a good point.

Some years I have nice surprises alongside my expensive harvest. Early one summer I noticed a couple of vines growing volunteer (meaning I did not plant them but they came up compliments of last year's compost). At first, I thought the vines were cucumbers, but as the blooms gave way to fruit they looked like gourds. Finally, the shape was unmistakably that of cantaloupe. While my tomatoes ran forty dollars apiece, that particular year I had four cantaloupes for free. This was not quite a financial wash, but I will take it.

Each spring I get over my failures in "the back forty" and plant again. In fact, long before spring arrives I will replace the summer crop with a winter one – collards and cabbage. Gardening is something one must do not merely for the end result – the harvest – but the journey or the process. There are other comparisons in life: we parent knowing there is really never a time we are finished (even though we may feel like giving up); one goes to work each day hopefully not just because retirement will come, but the satisfaction of doing a job that contributes to society; and following Jesus is not simply about getting to heaven, but believing the path here on earth is fulfilling too.

Why do you follow the Carpenter? Is it for the end results of eternal rewards or for the assurance of immediate gratifications like protection, peace, and a better parking place? There are many reasons – explicit and implicit – that Christians give for following Jesus. Perhaps there is none better than simply trusting that the journey is its own reward. In all of our bumps, bruises, disappointments, surprises and joys along the way, God is faithful. *And God is able to provide you with every blessing in abundance, so that by always having enough of everything, you may share abundantly in every good work.* (2 Corinthians 9:8)

Sometimes in life you go looking for tomatoes and end up finding cantaloupe, and life is good.

Part Two: The Long Trek
"A long obedience in the same direction…"
Friedrich Nietzsche

Have you ever heard a stone speak?

Oh, I have, many times. Rocks have memory and with memory there are stories to tell.

There are piles of rocks throughout the pastures and woods of our family's farm. They are the remains of chimneys from tenant farmers who lived on the place and scratched out a living chopping cotton, hoeing corn and milking cows. On one particular wood line are two piles of rocks; the only thing remaining of a house that no one in my family remembers when it was inhabited. Since the time Amy and I were dating we would walk among those rocks and dream of building our own house there. We would take some of those rocks and mark out the boundaries of the home and place stones along where we thought the chimney would be. It was our idea that we could use all those stones to make the fireplace.

We have moved on with our life and those dreams have given way to other realities. But whenever we are back home visiting, we try to find time to walk around the edge of those woods where cows graze and black birds call, and listen to those rocks, those stones that hold so much memory.

In the early pages of the book of Joshua we read about the children of Israel about to step into God's promise. They had longed for it; prayed for it; worked for it. And now it was before them. But before entering in, God instructed Joshua to take twelve rocks and stack them; twelve rocks that represent the twelve tribes of Israel. But they are not just a pile of river rocks. Joshua is told that when the children of Israel look upon this pile and are asked "what do these stones mean to you," they are to tell a story. They are to tell of what God has done for his children, how God has provided a way for them where there was none before.

They are not just a pile of rocks. They have a story to tell for those that are willing to listen.

When Israel looked to Jordan and saw those twelve stones they didn't just see another pile of rocks or a memorial to what God did in their past. Their children knew that they were rocks – anyone could see that. They wanted to know "what do these stones mean to you?" In other words, they wanted meaning. They wanted to know if the light that shone and broke forth in their history could shine anew in their time; they wanted to see that if God faithfully abided and led in the life of their ancestors, could God do it all over again, even when we are not so faithful.

Hiking on trails sometimes you see piles of rocks called cairns, particularly at places where a trail intersects with another. They not only symbolize those who have gone before, but they convey the message: "You are on the right path. Keep on trekking."

Literally and symbolically we are all leaving behind markers of where we have been; symbols of fidelity and, because we all stumble, unfaithfulness. Walking and wandering through this life is an opportunity to do so circumspectly, thoughtfully and compassionately. We pile up stones along the way not just to say, "I was here," but also to support those who follow behind us, that they may be gladdened in their journey and comforted by our historic presence.

Either way, when our trek is done, we will leave something behind. Will it be just a pile of rocks, destined to be scattered and forgotten? Or will we mark our path with hopeful and helpful signs for others in their life's journey?

Ancient stones telling ancient stories speak of God's fidelity and invite us to testimony, to a movement beyond a memory. May they cry out!

Dirty Pickup Trucks and Jesus

I am not known for clean cars. I like a clean car but most of the time my vehicle looks like a piece of discarded furniture parked between the lines. This may go back to the days when I owned a pick-up. It stayed on the muddy side. Imagine your pastor parking a muddy pickup outside of the church. Well, three congregations suffered the indignity of seeing my truck outside the church that looked like it was better suited to be parked outside of a honky-tonk. Rarely was it seen in public clean because my philosophy was that only *yuppies* (remember them? They are now replaced by hipsters, but I digress) have clean pickups. It was true that my truck was not the most professional looking vehicle in a funeral procession, but most of the time I rode with the funeral director, because my heater never worked.

I moved on from driving a truck to a MINI, but in time it began to look much like my former truck – caked in mud from dirt road excursions over weekend camping trips. Finally, I gave up trying to pretend that I can look dignified (even in a MINI), and bought a Jeep.

While I must apologize to those offended that my vehicle stays dirty more than it does clean, I make no apologies or excuses for anyone who chooses to keep their truck, Jeep, MINI, or skateboard, burnished with thick layers of Georgia clay. Besides, trucks and Jeeps are supposed to look *used*. That is what they are for.

At the end of the day I believe we are supposed to look a little used too. Woe to the one who goes through life clean as a whistle, never dirtying their hands with the "stuff of life." We are put here to get used up in the service of loving others. I love the image in John's gospel where Jesus takes off his "party jacket" and roles his sleeves up to wash feet.

In an age of antiseptic gel and SUVs that have never seen a dirt road, Jesus seems to be saying if you want to follow me – get dirty. Jesus tells stories about victims cast on the side of the road; lepers in need of a gentle touch of hope; the dead having a life given back to them; and spittle-soaked mud that anointed eyes and restored sight.

Jesus believed that the Gospel – the good news – comes with dirty feet, pierced hands, and tear-stained embraces. Fresh sanctuaries with light filtered through stained glass is pretty and has its place, but the real work is "out there."

Do something with your faith today: forgive an enemy, love a stranger, give to someone without them knowing it. No doubt you will get dirtied up from it, but that is the point.

Burial Ground of the Stars

If you're planning a visit to Los Angeles, you might want to swing by *The Hollywood Forever Cemetery* -- the burial ground of the stars. Since it opened more than a 100 years ago, the cemetery has become the last resting place of the likes of Cecil B. DeMille, Douglas Fairbanks, Tyrone Power and Marion Davies. There is one grave with a dog carved out of granite perched on the top. It belongs (well, I guess "belong" is too possessive of a word for someone who is dead) to "Alfalfa" from *The Little Rascals*. He was killed over a dispute with his dog – it was a different dog than "Petey."

Their eccentric owner neglected the once glorious grounds and by the 1990s, *The Hollywood Forever Cemetery* suffered bankruptcy and a buy-out. The new owner is now offering a novel product to the mortal - the chance to plan exactly how you will be remembered -- through video biographies.

How do you want to be remembered? Probably not like "Alfalfa" with a granite dog staring at you for all eternity. I once owned a beloved Labrador Retriever named Samson, who would stare at me every morning around 4:30 am. Pretty creepy. I am not too sure about a video biography either. They say the camera adds 10 pounds and there is not much I can do about my face without employing a good airbrush artist. The thought of being buried next to a famous Hollywood star doesn't thrill me either. It is not like you can socialize in a cemetery.

The truth is, beyond a generation or two most of us will not be remembered. What we do, however, can have a lasting impact. The liturgical calendar reflects different ways in which we can respond to God's "inburst" into this world. Take Advent and Christmas, for example. No one knows the names of the shepherds who heard the angels and gathered around the manger. What we do know is that they were touched by God's love and they told the story. For every generation since then the story has been retold.

Poet Ann Weems writes:

When the Holy Child is born into our hearts
There is a rain of stars
A rushing of angels
A blaze of candles
This God bursts into our lives.
Loving is running through the streets.

Give a lasting legacy by telling and living the story. It is much more enduring than a granite marker or a video biography.

Better Boys Among Us

The last few years my reputation as a farmer has greatly suffered. Of course, that is assuming I had a reputation as a farmer in the first place. I have planted and labored in the fields only to find that deer and other varmints beat me to the harvest or droughts beat down my plants or insects beat down my hopes. It is enough to make a preacher…well, you understand. It is not like I have flowing pastures of excess to watch over. Really it is just a couple of small raised beds, and three containers. Therefore, every squash counts and every tomato is special (and expensive).

Some years my vigilance pays off. Maybe it happens when I use the "nasty" spray that repels deer, varmints, traveling evangelists and my wife from entering the back yard. Every so often, there are harvest seasons when I am delighted to report that there are Better Boys among us – nice, ripe, fat, juicy tomatoes that make their way to the supper table.

Some say the summer begins when school ends for the year. Others remark that it does not really begin until the neighborhood pool is open. Still others mark the beginning of summer with Memorial Day, while technically it does not arrive until Summer Solstice. For me summer begins with the first ripe tomato.

All gardening involves hope and trust. At some point, you do all you can then you have to trust to the earth what you have planted and hope that it will come to fruition. Many times, it ends in disappointment and sometimes it exceeds expectations.

I love that line from Jesus when he compares the Kingdom of God to someone who goes out and plants seeds "…and would sleep and rise night and day, and the seed would sprout and grow, he does not know how." I approach gardening like most everything else in life: *what else do I need to do?* Jesus celebrates the farmer who, after the sweat and work, goes to sleep. At some point, there is nothing else you can do but trust and hope and leave it, in a somewhat Pelagian way, up to God to bring about the growth.

Growing is a gift, a grace. It also means an act of trust and faith will be involved.

Peter Rhea Jones wrote: "Part of Christian discipleship is letting God work." (*The Teaching of the Parables*, p. 107) Our role in this journey is planting and harvesting. The growth is a gift, an act of grace.

What is it in your life that you need to trust over to God and all that is left is to wait with hope? I know that all of life needs to be trusted over to God, yet so often I fret, I worry, and I think "if I can just do one more thing." At some point, however, I need to hand it over: my family, my ambitions, my vocation, my life – everything.

The rest is up to God and what God has begun, God will bring to a triumphant conclusion.

A Little Walt Whitman is Good for the Soul ...

I dream'd in a dream I saw a city invincible,
  to the attacks of the whole of the rest of the earth,
I dream'd that was the new city of Friends.

I keep a copy of Whitman's *Leaves of Grass* on the end table by my reading chair. I read snatches of his lines in the early morning before digging into whatever book I am working through at the time. There is just something about those 19th century American Romantics that have me returning to their waters time and again to drink. Another American Romantic, Henry David Thoreau, has a wondrous line or two in his most famous work, "Walden." In the opening pages, he writes:

> *I went to the woods because I wished to live deliberately; to front only the essentials in life and see what it had to teach me. And not, when I came to die, discover that I had never lived.*

Those few words make me want to grab my walking stick leaning in a corner of my house and head out to the wooded hills with my wife in hand to see what there is to see. The words of Whitman and Thoreau have lasted so long because they speak to the heart of the human condition – the desire to live faithfully and deliberately. It is also a reminder of the importance of abiding together.

It is part of the church's responsibility to bear upon our consciences that God created us to live not in isolation but in community, and to do so with a holy intentionality. So many – too many – trudge through life going through the mechanics of work, family, responsibilities and other routines and fail to actually live. The Bible reminds us that we each play an important and significant role:

> *As it is, there are many members, yet one body ... [25] that there may be no dissension within the body, but the members may have the same care for one another. [26] If one member suffers, all suffer together*

> *with it; if one member is honored, all rejoice together with it.* (1 Corinthians 12:20, 25-26)

My prayer for the Church – the global communion of saints as well as the local community of faith - is two-fold: 1) that each of us as we sojourn discover how indispensable we really are in the community, and 2) that each we live lives fully, abundantly and faithfully. And when we falter, may we live in the generosity of God's grace for another day.

I am grateful to be a part.

Fragments of a Life

Tiny scraps of paper were scattered about the floor of my small study at home. My first inclination was to pick up the little pieces and toss the debris in the trash. Well, actually, my *very* first thought was to ignore the litter and pretend I didn't see the mess and leave it for another, more convenient time. I thought better of the first thought, so I stooped down and started picking up the little tatters of paper. No doubt this was a small mess created by our little girl Annie – a bullboxer puppy we adopted from a rescue shelter one summer. Picking up the pieces I noticed that it was a photograph she nibbled away from the bookshelf. I am sure she thought, "That guy in the picture looks nice…I think I will bite his face and maybe digest a few parts."

The picture was from a 1992 whitewater trip I led with a group from the church I served as pastor. I was 26 when the photo was taken, and my oldest child (not pictured) was only a few months old. There I was in the snapshot (or what was now left of me): young and confident; hopeful and expectant. Twenty-four years later I can say that I still like a good paddle down a river, but I am not so young and that little boy of mine is now nearly as old as I was in the photo.

I am a bit sad that there is not much left of the picture. What Annie left me is more like a cheap puzzle missing several pieces. Still, even what was left among the fragments brought back sweet memories of a life I lived with a people I served in the mountains I love.

Even the best pictures we have are never whole; never complete; and can in no way tell the whole story. For that matter, the same could be said of our memories. They too are never whole, complete, nor tell the whole story. All we are left with are our fragments.

Through the years these fragments weave in and out and make a life. Or, put another way, a life is made out of all our fragments - good and tragic; joys and sadness; struggles and triumphs. No life is a whole life until we have lived all of our life.

I look back with gratitude even over the parts I would rather forget or never have lived. I am grateful that no one fragment defines me; it only is a part of me. I am much bigger than the sum of my fragments.

So are you.

May you look ahead at the outstretched river you are navigating through with gratitude for where you have been and hope for where you are going. The picture is not yet complete.

The boundary lines have fallen for me in pleasant places; I have a goodly heritage. (Psalm 16:6)

Pressing forward.

What Does God Look Like?

Every child wants to know, and many have the courage to ask, "What does God look like?" The adult in all of us wants to quickly answer in a theologically correct way, saying knowingly, "God cannot be pictured. An image is idolatrous because no one image can ever be complete." Still, the child in all of us wants to know, "what *does* God look like?"

When I was in high school my art teacher shocked my naive prejudices when he showed me a photograph of a mural he painted for his church. The scene included a depiction of Jesus. In his painting Jesus had ebony black skin and wiry afro. This was no Jesus like I had ever seen. Yet it was very much Jesus to my art teacher and his church.

Some see God as a triumphant king or a valiant warrior. Others see God as an ethereal mystery, elusive and distant. There are those that see God as a manifestation of Western values while others picture God only in the Southern Hemisphere.

What does God look like to you?

Look in the mirror. In Genesis are the words: *"So God created humankind in his image, in the image of God he created them; male and female he created them."* God is etched in our faces – young and old, shaded in a variety of pigments, reflected in our wholeness and brokenness.

What is idolatrous is when we attempt to contain God in a singular or exclusive image. That is why when places of worship gather, it is best and ideal when the gathering reflects a community of diversity. In our differences, we "image" a better picture of who God is in our community and in our world.

We see God at work all over this world in faces of others, as well as in our own face. Our mission is to join with God in that holy enterprise, bearing image and bearing witness.

There are times the work of God takes us no further than the local church, worshipping and celebrating in a variety of forms and traditions. In this community of diverse images, we can gaze into the ancient texts to read how others "beheld the Glory," and seek to discern more about how to live faithfully in a complex world.

But God is also at work all over the world and so we cannot stay put, looking at each other. We are created to be verbs, imaging God at work and witness. We go to serve and work and listen and dwell with our neighbors; discovering how the Spirit of God is at work next door and around the world.

It is a beautiful thought isn't it: God's wonderful, diverse family united by a common devotion to follow and see Jesus wherever God is at work.

Whatever you think the face of God might look like; I assure you that your face is welcome as well! After all, you reflect God's image too.

Walking Across the Street One Sunday

It was a difficult summer in 2015. Emmanuel African Methodist Episcopal Church in Charleston experienced unthinkable violence in the name of racial hatred. Nine members, including the pastor, were dead, and the rest of the nation was wounded. We all knew it was horrific. We all knew it was drenched in hate. We came to know too, that in spite of the intended racial division, we witnessed great acts of charity and forgiveness.

What I did not know, however, were the neighbors right across the street of the church I served as pastor. Right across from my magnificent church I served for over a decade is a smaller congregation that sits in the shadow of the giant steeple. Gardner Grove Baptist Church is primarily an African-American congregation. They are not particularly prominent or large in number. Maybe that was why I had not encountered my neighbors. I did know they were faithful. Sundays and Wednesdays their parking lot was always full, as well as other days when there was a wedding or funeral or some other special event.

Still, after ten years I had never met our neighbors across the street from my church. Following the Charleston massacre, I knew it was long overdue for me to meet my neighbors. Between worship services the week after the massacre I walked across the hot asphalt street that divides our congregations and entered the foyer of their sanctuary. They were well into worship, so I was sensitive to the fact that my presence would be conspicuous as well as an interruption to their service. I left a card with the sound technician to give to the pastor that said something to the effect, "I am sorry about the racial hatred of our times. We need to get to know each other."

The next day their pastor and I exchanged calls followed by a visit. Though we shared "Baptist" in our church names, denominationally our affiliations are different. I am guessing there are other differences too. Yet we were happily united in a common devotion of faith and a common hope for our community and world. He said to me, "What happened in Charleston will not divide us. It has the opportunity to unite us." We made a commitment to not only get to know each other better, but for our congregations to get to know each other better. We are neighbors after all and that is what neighbors do. In the weeks after that meeting, many church members would cross the street to worship with the brothers and sisters of Gardner Grove.

I wish there were words that I could share that would resolve the racial strife we are still experiencing in our land and in our time. I wish I could articulate a better vision of what could be. I wish I had the acumen to devise a plan, a program, or a response that could augment lasting healing. All I can really do is meet my neighbors and move from being a stranger to a friend. I can walk across the many different streets that divide races, religions, socio-economic classes, politics, and extend a hand and be a friend.

You can walk across the street too, and I think it needs to be just that literal. If you do not know your neighbors, then make a moment to walk across whatever it is that divides you from another and bring a card, or flowers, or a cake, or just a genuine smile and say, "It's good to meet you." Some neighbors we cannot meet due to geography or circumstances beyond our control. Such divisions are seemingly insurmountable. But you can still get to know your neighbors by listening, learning and praying for compassion and empathy. Do not meet a neighbor intending to tell them what they need to know about you. Meet your neighbor to learn something new about them. It will change both of you.

The Bible is particularly sensitive to the importance of neighborliness. From the laws of the Old Testament to the teachings of Jesus; caring, protecting, and showing mercy to the neighbor is how others see God at work in this world. Politics and acts of Congress will not make this happen. We can change our symbols and our laws but if we do not change our hearts and actions it will all be useless.

Walk across the street and get to know your neighbor. You just might meet a friend.

"...You shall love the Lord your God with all your heart, and with all your soul, and with all your mind, and with all your strength.' The second is this, 'You shall love your neighbor as yourself.' There is no other commandment greater than these." (Mark 12:30-31)

Pork Skins and Diet Coke

I am not much of a "snacker." Food is too important to me to just treat lightly or delicately. I am an unapologetic vegetarian-except-when-eating-meat eater. Still, a snack is not a bad thing if it tides me over until the next meal. With apologies to my many kosher friends, one of my favorite snacks are pork skins and a close second would be pork rinds followed by pork cracklings (if you do not know what cracklings are you must not be from the south). I like to wash down all this savory, salty goodness with a diet coke, because I am, after all, concerned with my calorie intake. Along with my physician you may be relieved to know I do not engage too often in snacking. It is a weakness of mine when I am traveling.

There are few things that are lovelier when driving along some of the great back roads in Georgia than signs advertising pork skins or "boiled p-nuts." You know it is going to be good if the word "peanuts" is misspelled. While I like all kinds of food, common, basic food always hits the spot. Given a choice between collards and spinach soufflé' and I will choose the collards every time.

Like fried chicken and biscuits, the basics are the best.

As people of faith we are tempted to listen to the latest and greatest ideas and purveyors of trends, but neglect the basics of a life together: community, study, prayer, fellowship. Before buildings and budgets and committees; before staff and clergy and mission statements, it was the basics that anchored the early church in the "fifth gospel" called Acts. And long before the first century church, these same basics held the treasured possession called Israel as they made their way through wilderness and into the land promised to them. And when the covenant was broken and they were driven into exile and diaspora, the basics of community, study, prayer and fellowship kept them centered while displaced.

Even those not familiar with communities of faith know that organized religion is in an era of great, even seismic change. Still, we are trekking ever onward into the *Missio Dei* – the Mission or Work of God. Now as always, we that are on this great journey must time and again renew our commitments to God's mission through the community of faith and we best not neglect the basics along the way. Here are four simple things we can do for cultivating the faith:

- Commit to worship with a community of believers. Common devotion allows us to also share our common concerns and fear.
- Commit to the study of scripture, both personal and corporate. Discerning ancient words is both a personal responsibility, and a communal privilege to listen to how others experience the text.
- Commit to sharing financially with others that can help accomplish both a local and global mission. All that we have is a gift; therefore, let us live in such a way that we give everything away.
- Commit to serving your neighbor in tangible and loving ways. The neighbor is a friend or family; but also, the stranger and the guest.

Basic stuff, I know, but it is the basics that have held us together through the generations.

Our Place in this World

There is one thing we all share in this world – for better or for worse, we all come from a family. Families shape us and mold us and are the singular most influential force in our life. Some of the most enduring images of God are birthed out of our experiences with our mothers and fathers.

Some families take interest in learning about their family histories. Over the years I have asked questions, done some research, and listened to the stories as shared by my "elders." The stories I like best are the sensational and scintillating ones that have passed through the generations with a bit of embellishment added in the passage of time. My great-great grandfather, for example, was arrested on Christmas Eve for swindling someone out of fifty cents. Today it is a humorous story. At the time, I feel certain it was not so funny. He was the same guy that shot the locks off a church door just to get out of a revival meeting – or at least that is how the story has been passed down through the years. All of the eye-witnesses are long gone from this world.

On one of my hikes up in the Great Smoky Mountains I took a side trail that was not on the map. It had to lead somewhere, or so I thought, and so I hoofed up it, zig-zagging through the woods, going up, down, and through ravines, and numerous bends along the path, until I finally round a corner to a small level place of ground. It was dotted with headstones, primarily unmarked, of an old family cemetery. These were folks "left behind" as mountaineers left the land when it was established as a National Park. It was hard to tell if there were any family still making visits to this old cemetery hidden in the mountains.

Families can give us orientation and they can also create disorientation. We want to know answers to fundamental questions, "Where did I come from?" in order to better understand "How did I get here?" These lead to further questions such as, "Where do I want to go?" and "How do I plan to get there?"

Churches are a larger expression of the family, and so together we ask similar questions: *Where did we come from? How did we get here? Where do we want to go? How do we plan to get there?*

These are questions of orientation and theologically we call this the language of prayer. Prayer at its basic, most elemental form is the mystical search for orientation – finding our place in this world. Some of the most enduring images of Jesus are those when he would separate himself from work and from others in order to find orientation:

Now during those days, he went out to the mountain to pray; and he spent the night in prayer to God.
(Luke 6:12)

Wherever you are in life, it is a privilege to share life with you, together, in this family of faith. Let us now seek together not only our place in this world, but our place with our Creator, Sustainer, Comforter, and Friend.

Not-so-pleasant Surprises

One summer evening, when the air was typically heavy in a gauzy mix of humidity and dust, I was cutting grass along the shoulder of the road in front of our house. Meanwhile my neighbor across the street was in his front yard cutting down a dead tree and sectioning it to haul away. Out of the corner of my eye I noticed he quickly dropped one of the logs, so I assumed he might need a neighborly hand. When I crossed the street, he looked at me and said, "I think there is a snake with a bird in the log." I am no expert in herpetology or ornithology, but I am pretty sure snakes and birds do not nest together. After my own inspection, my neighbor was correct: a king snake was coiled around the remains of a bird. The snake looked annoyed, but the bird was no longer complaining. Apparently, the bird flew into the hollow of the tree and was surprised by this visitor for dinner.

The next morning when I left for work I noticed my neighbor still had that log sitting in his front yard, presumably with the snake still ensconced in it, digesting its meal. As I recall, that particular log remained in his front yard for most, if not all, that summer.

Not-so-pleasant surprises come in all forms: snakes in the grass; yellow-jackets in the shrubbery; or bats in the eaves. I suppose at times it feels like nature is working against us, but then again nature usually does what it is supposed to do. It is neither for us nor against us.

What about our nature; how do we live and act according to *our* nature? The evidence is mixed. We pollute the earth and our bodies; we exact great harm upon others out of vengeance; we repackage envy and call it ambition; and we revision greed and name it a virtue.

And yet…it is also our nature that we bear the image of God. This in itself is too marvelous to understand, but can be seen if we pay attention. I see in others great acts of sacrifice, not because it can be defended economically, but out of a deep and mysterious love. I witness bold stances on truth and justice, even though it may bring derision and ridicule.

A few years ago, I read a story about a monk rescuing a scorpion from a spider web. The monk would reach to disentangle the scorpion, but would get stung in the process. Still the monk continued until finally the scorpion was set free. One of the novices asked the monk, "Why did you try to save the scorpion, when you knew it was going to sting you?" The monk replied, "It is the scorpion's nature to kill; it is my nature to save."

Some say it is in our nature that sin abounds, and I suppose this is true. The testimony of our planet is evidence enough. But I say God has created us for more than to abide according to our lesser nature. We are image-bearers of the Holy.

Let's surprise the world with something better than what we are seeing!

In God's Immutable Love,

Muffin Top Drop

That was the subject line of an email I recently received. I am not sure if it was a promotion for weight-loss or advertising a delicious pastry. I decided to forgo opening the email, assuming it was unsolicited. Besides, I like muffin tops and I do not need an email to convince me of it.

I am amazed at the emails that get filtered and never make it to my virtual desk and those emails, like the one I mention above, that make it through in spite of our filters. For example, today I received unsolicited emails promoting cigars, credit reports, memory loss prevention and something called a "belly buster." (I hope my emails are not some kind of profile) When I accessed my junk file that automatically redirects emails from my inbox, I found emails from church members wondering why I had not replied to earlier emails; a poetry blog I subscribed to years ago; and something from Harvard (I am sure it was a delayed acceptance letter).

Some people I know could stand to work on their filters. Saying and posting whatever comes to mind or how one is feeling at a time of heightened emotions is rarely a wise choice. God gave to us a frontal lobe and while not all lobes are created equal, a little reflection before speaking or writing is good for the soul and good for others too.

Should churches ever filter? Apparently, we try to with our server, but you see how effective that is. No, no, I mean should churches ever filter who is welcome and who is? Think before you answer…Is everyone really accepted here, unfiltered, just as they are?

I wonder, worry actually, about those that are filtered out from the church. I know that we do not always intend to filter others out, but nevertheless it happens. Our dress, our language, our innocent "cliques" can set up filters that make it difficult for others to enter in. Some of our ideologies may also stand in the way. Political opinions, judgmental declarations, and daily dramas can be formidable filters that are difficult to get past.

Jesus tells a story in Matthew of a king hosting a wedding banquet and when the invited guests do not show, he opens the doors to everyone. "Go therefore into the main streets, and invite everyone you find to the wedding banquet" (22:9). It is a great picture of what the kingdom of God looks like: a radically inclusive place where the hurting and dispossessed have a place at the table. The story takes a strange turn, however, when someone shows up without proper dress – a robe – and is summarily kicked out to the streets.

At first glance, this seems rather harsh. Does it really matter in this story whether or not the guy has on the "right" clothes? But this story is not about proper clothing. It is an allegory. The man accepted the invitation of the gospel, "but refused to conform his life to the gospel." (Douglas Hare)

We are called and loved without filters, but we are claimed with great expectations. We enter in singing "Just as I am," but we go out never the same again.

No longer can bigotry of any kind be "unfiltered", for Jesus said, "Love your neighbor."

No longer do our personal rights take "unfiltered" priority, for Jesus said, "The greatest among you will be your servant."

No longer will our greed be permitted "unfiltered", for Jesus said, "What good is it to gain the whole world but lose your soul?"

The dialectical tension of the Gospel is that we are loved and welcomed without filters and yet we are changed and transformed to live, love and do differently. The church, God's community here on earth, is not a place where we go to have our own ideas and biases supported and enforced. Church is where we enter unfiltered and sent transformed by the call, the invitation of Christ.

How is God's good news *changing* me? That is the question I am asking of me. I think it is a big enough question to share with you, unfiltered.

In-Between Addresses

Throughout our marriage Amy and I have always enjoyed a place to call home. Our first home was small garage apartment (are any of them large?). Our largest home was a pastorium in Chickamauga – a five-bedroom split-level. A few times we lived "in-between addresses." I know that sounds odd, but I can find no better way to describe such a living situation.

One of those in-between addresses to serve a church and while we shopped for a house, we lived for several months in their missionary house. The last time was a few months before moving to another city. Our house quickly sold and so we hastily rented a house to spend Thanksgiving and Christmas and New Year's Eve.

For that last move, living in-between addresses meant that most of our worldly goods were packed up and in storage, including eight boxes of Christmas decorations that accumulated over the years. Initially it felt as though this may be the year without a Christmas.

Thanks to online searching, Amy found a recipe for cookie dough ornaments: cinnamon, applesauce, and glue. They smell wonderful, but take my word for it, you do not want to eat one! The irony is that nearly three decades prior we were doing the same thing, but with a different recipe, for our first Christmas – making cookie dough ornaments for our first Christmas together. You make do, with what you have. That year, along with some ribbon and craft acrylics, we decorated our freshly baked ornaments, strung a couple of strands of lights on a modest tree bought at a grocery store and at a total cost of about $40 Christmas has come to our "in-between address."

I suppose we all are living in-between addresses. We move from a past that can never be recovered and into a future that is anything but certain. All we have is the in-between times, the meantime, the beautiful and mysterious now. Advent is that cosmic pause in a universe moving rapidly from one space to the next. Mary and Joseph scuttle south heading to Bethlehem, pausing along the way to find shelter and a manger in the night. Far from home, Jesus is born homeless, a refugee in a greedy empire and an indifferent public.

Blessed is the innkeeper, nameless and for some scorned, for making a place in a stable.

Blessed is Joseph, who kept the faith and provided against all other evidence.

Blessed is Mary, who believed knowing that it would one day cost her what was most precious.

Blessed are all those who find beauty while in-between addresses, believing that it is not where you are from or even where you are going that matters most, but where you are right now. And wherever you are, hang an ornament, call it good, and invite others to see and find joy.

In a darkened sky, field hands far away from home looked up and saw a heavenly host, celestial ornaments of that first Christmas of in-between addresses, singing, "Glory to God in the highest, and on earth peace, good will toward all…" (Luke 2:14)

Enough

One year in the middle of our annual vacation to the beach, my boys arose early in the morning to leave early, heading back to their respective apartments, to work, and to their friends. As I was hugging them bye and seeing them off, I thought about how it never seems to be "enough" with my boys who are now young men. Never enough time…enough play…enough work…enough hours in the day…enough love…enough rest…enough money…enough faith…enough laughter…enough intelligence…enough friends.

Why is it, I wondered at the edge of the dunes watching my boys drive away, that scarcity seems to be the one thing we have enough of? At work and home and play, we are more defined by what we do not have enough of than what is truly enough.

Even church does not escape this culture of scarcity. Never enough in the budget…enough teachers in Sunday School…enough laps in the nursery…enough visits to the elderly…enough activities for the students…enough clarity of faith…enough worshippers on Sunday…enough fried chicken on Wednesday!

Maybe that is why some of the most memorable stories in the Bible are those that confront scarcity. Moses calls for bread from heaven and water from the rock to provide in the barren wilderness. Elijah depressed and alone, meets God not in the mighty acts of earthquake or fire, but in the still small voice. Jesus holds up a few loaves and fish and feeds the multitude. Somehow in the scarcity there is provision. There is enough.

Can you allow yourself the grace of enough even in your scarcity? Your love and worth is not measured by the number of likes on Facebook or Instagram, but by the One who made all things and said it is very good – it is *enough!* Because we are not whole, we will never be able to love enough, forgive enough, or show mercy enough. Therefore, we must risk ourselves with each other that in our scarcity God will be enough – enough love, enough forgiveness, enough mercy.

And when we find out that enough is enough, we find peace, we find gratitude, we find hope. We find out it is enough.

For God alone my soul waits in silence; from him comes my salvation. He alone is my rock and my salvation, my fortress; I shall never be shaken. (Psalm 62)

Does Your Well Hold Water?

Like many of you, I grew up depending on wells for my water and the thought of paying someone else for water was ridiculous. The only people I thought that paid for water were naïve city slickers who get talked into snipe hunting and refer to "cokes" as "sodas."

The old well that supported the dairy and my grandparent's house also had the luxury of an electric pump that was added when my daddy was a child. The well itself, if I remember correctly, was dug by hand by my grandfather. In spite of the electric pump, however, the well was not always reliable. Many nights I was sent to cross through the pasture of sleeping cows and prime the pump because the water level had dropped too low. By the time I was well into my teens the old well had been replaced with a new, professionally drilled well that goes down some 300 feet.

Throughout the pastures and woods where I grew up there are several old wells, many of them are virtually forgotten. Some have been filled in with rock and debris, but there are at least two that are still open and exposed. They are relatively shallow and now bone dry.

Empty wells have long been used as a metaphor for life. Early in his prophetic oracle against Israel, Jeremiah spoke on behalf of God: "…they have forsaken me, the fountain of living water, and dug out **cisterns** for themselves, cracked **cisterns** that can hold no water" (Jeremiah 2:13). I do not know much about cisterns, but I get the point.

Does your well hold water? Have you been pursuing all the wrong things and now find yourself coming up empty? That can probably be said of all of us. My suggestion would be to prime your pump or dig a little deeper. In other words, keep the main thing the main thing: Love God, love yourself, love your neighbor. Now that is a well and a life that will hold water!

Baptizing Kevin

Kevin's mom approached me and abruptly said, "I think Kevin is ready for baptism." It is certainly not uncommon for me to hear from parents of twelve-year-old boys this type of request. But this request was anything but common.

Kevin is a child with significant developmental disabilities. He was born premature, which plays a role in his disabilities. For the first two years of his life – the most important for development - Kevin was tragically neglected, which only exacerbated his disabilities. By God's grace and love Kevin was adopted. I still remember when Kevin was brought to church for the first time. He could not talk, walk or even crawl. He whimpered and required near constant care.

"What are we going to do about Kevin?" I heard others ask. All of us – from workers in the nursery to ministers on staff – felt unqualified and helpless against Kevin's formidable challenges. What we did was love Kevin, just as he was, and in the process discovered how deeply we were loved by him.

Through the years we watched Kevin grow up, so to speak. We watched him learn to crawl and then toddle and before long lumber around the classrooms and church grounds. He went from whimpering to smiling. In time, he began to speak a word or two, then phrases, and now he can easily share a sentence with you when something is on his mind – and something is always on his mind! In preschool and later children's choir, we watched him stand alongside his peers while an adult held him by the belt to help him keep balance or keep him from ambling away. Kevin did not always know the words, nor keep proper tempo, but he nearly always smiled as he sung the words that mattered to him. And because they mattered to him they mattered to us.

Kevin is now a 6th grader, but he just cannot move about, play or interact quite like his peers. Sometimes all he can do is just sit, while a whirlwind of busy adolescents swirl around him. Just as often, however, his classmates will not let him sit, and so he gets drawn up into the activity too.

No, Kevin will never really understand what is meant by the words, "Jesus is Lord," but then again, who among us does? So, when his mother talked with me about Kevin getting baptized, I realized that I needed to change how I think of baptism and what it means to be fully included in the community of faith. You see in some ways preparing for baptism involves understanding basic doctrines of the Christian faith, especially regarding salvation. It is important, at least that has been my thinking, to understand that baptism involves entering the deadly waters, dying to self and being raised up to walk in a new life with Christ. But what if you do not understand it at all? Who among us really does? Baptism is not simply a transformation of the mind. It is a changing of the heart. Over the years not only has Kevin's heart changed, ours have changed too.

On the Fourth Sunday of Advent, after six others entered and exited the baptismal waters, along came Kevin, surrounded by three men who watched, supported, and loved this little boy through his years with the church. Kevin could not get the words quite right when he was supposed to say, "Jesus is Lord," and his immersion was a bit clumsy and piecemeal. Technically speaking, some parts of Kevin are a bit, shall we say, "unbaptized." Still, Kevin taught us all that morning that belonging to the community of faith is not about what you know in your head. It is who you know in your heart. He taught us that love comes not from an intellectual enterprise. It comes from a place of trust.

Through the years Kevin was taught that Jesus is Lord and loves us as we are. In God's cosmic mystery, that is exactly what Kevin taught us. We are all learning together.

I am grateful for my teacher Kevin.

Am I My Brother's Keeper?

I am the older of my two brothers. One is just 10 ½ months younger (so we share the same numerical age for six bemusing weeks) and the other, the baby of the family, is 2 ½ years younger. We are close in age and growing up we were fierce in loyalty. I should add that we were, from time to time through adolescence, just as fierce antagonizing each other, tussling through our childhood as brothers tend to do.

There is a well-known story in Genesis of two brothers, Cain and Abel, sons of Adam and Eve. Cain harbors anger against his brother Abel that escalates. Inexplicably Cain kills his brother. Immediately in the story we read that the LORD asked Cain, "Where is your brother?" Cain retorts, "Am I my brother's keeper?" (Genesis 4:9)

Although the question is not answered, we know the answer, don't we? "Yes, yes Cain, you are your brother's keeper." And so am I and so are you. We are our brother's and our sister's keeper.

Yet much too often we abide more in the isolation with Cain, absorbed in self – pity, narcissism, greed, and anxiety. Cain loses a brother because he was looking out for himself, forgetting that his identity is shared with others. In losing his brother he loses himself.

We neglect our brothers and sisters in so many small acts. On Facebook, we "unfriend" those whose words are inconvenient; we objectify according to gender, race, socio-economics; and we selfishly consume conspicuously because of our steady-belief in the god of scarcity. Who has time for watching out for brothers and sisters while looking out for #1? When you believe only in looking out for yourself, only trusting in yourself, and fearing for yourself, you reject any notion that you are your brother's keeper.

In a recent newspaper article, I was reminded of the late Jewish theologian Martin Buber, who wrote a seminal work in 1938, *I and Thou*. Buber writes that we are created in relationship, but when we treat others as objects to be used, vilified, exploited, or neglected we diminish our sacred birthright. The "Thou" of the other is reduced to "it."

Missions is a way to meet God in the world and discover God has given us work to do for the common good. We keep each other, brothers and sisters, as Martin Luther King, Jr. wrote, "tied together in a single garment of destiny."

One day God will ask of us, "where is your brother…where is your sister?" Our life will be the answer, but I hope we will have something more to say than Cain's anxious response.

Thankful to be peacefully kept by many

An Inconvenient Truth

There is so much good to say about the church. Through the years I have published articles, written sermons, and publicly and passionately advocated for churches. Goodness, to be really candid, for the last thirty or so years I have made my living working for churches.

But there is an inconvenient truth: sometimes, perhaps much of the time, church and church members can be difficult. Sometimes church and church members can be painful. One person commented recently that she could never seem to fit into any of the observable cliques that she saw in the churches she visited. She knew there was good there, but could never seem to be included in that good.

I get it, I really do.

Deep in our humanity is the need to find community. We live not in isolation, but in relationships. Communities, however, can quickly become closed groups. In a provincial sense of the word, communities can become cliques. This is when communities get twisted, mutated, and fearful. Maybe we do not mean to be, but it easier to turn our backs on others, because we are more comfortable with the familiar.

In my neighborhood live several families from Turkey. The old grandfather, hobbled by age and arthritis, speaks very little English. When I am out walking my dog, he will give me a small, toothless smile, while clutching his cane in one hand and his rosary beads in another. His children are much more comfortable with the language, although they still struggle for the right words when we exchange brief pleasantries. Their children, however, "fit right in." I assume they were born in this country and so things like language, dress, and sports – what can be called "culture" – helps them adjust in a way that their grandfather will never know. Of course, if I were to move to Turkey my plight would be the same as his. I am glad they are finding a place and I am grateful to share a small part of that place with them.

There is an inconvenient truth that churches can be closed: close-minded; isolated; irrelevant; fearful; and exclusive. Here I am not simply talking about ethnic diversity, although that is not a bad place to start. I am talking about anyone who is "different" – economically; socially; emotionally; intellectually; politically…this list could go on and on.

We who go to church and practice church and believe in the church have a responsibility to confess where we have failed to be good neighbors of welcome and commit to practicing a higher truth.

Jesus opened his arms wide and said: "Come unto me all who are weary…" Weary is another word for tired. Many are tired of church, so we have work to do to be the living incarnation of the Body of Christ inviting a tired world to find rest, a place to go to, a people to belong to, and where there is always room at the table for one more.

May the inconvenient truth be transformed to The Truth, The Way, and The Life.

A Spare or a Prayer

One fall day I was in North Georgia plowing through a forest service road looking for a spot to pitch a tent and count some stars. To the uninformed and uninitiated, a forest service road is off the beaten path of the comparatively tame asphalt byways. This particular road carves through a national forest used by campers, hikers and I assume national forest workers (although I have never seen the latter). The road was, well, challenging - packed dirt, loose rocks, with divots, holes, and the occasional carcass of something that did not make it across the road. A few miles into the ride, just around the bend, my tire pressure light lit up on the dash panel indicating I was losing pressure fast. This was not a good place to have a flat tire – miles away from anyone and well out of cell phone coverage. Of course, is there ever a good place to have a flat?

Well into jacking up the jeep, and fumbling with the spare, a mountain biker chugged by and offered to help. "I am fine," I said, wondering just what help a dude on his bicycle could actually provide. Soon a truck ambled by and its driver also offered to lend a hand. "No thank you," I answered, now confessing gratitude that on this lonely road there were folks willing and able to help if needed. I was grateful too to have both a spare and a prayer.

A spare and a prayer; these are the tools to help get the job done and inspiration to see it through.

What about those who do not have either: a spare or a prayer? Know anyone like that? Life has come unhinged, things have fallen apart, and they are stuck on the side of the road. Not only do we know people like that, at different points in time we all come up short without either a spare or a prayer.

Thanks be to God for those who peddle alongside us offering the hand, the word, the prayer to get us out of the ditch and back rolling again. Thanks be to God for the caregiver, the nurse, the teacher, the doctor, the sales clerk, the senior, the child, the friend who takes time to slow down and reach out and love.

Do you have a spare and a prayer? Then give thanks and look for the one who has not. You just might save a life and help heal a soul.

Beloved, let us love one another, because love is from God; everyone who loves is born of God and knows God...God's love was revealed among us in this way: God sent his only Son into the world so that we might live through him. (1 John 4:7, 9)

Loved and blessed.

A Selfish Article

The term "selfie" is a rather new word in our culture, and, by my own observations, fairly common. It refers to taking a self-portrait, usually with one's phone. Some take pictures of themselves by standing in front of a mirror, which in my opinion is quite strange since the camera is now part of the portrait. The other method – my preferred technique – is to extend the arm holding the camera and click the picture. Many would agree that the longer the arm, according to the rules of perspective, the better the portrait. With a selfie-stick you can take the camera out another couple of feet and actually take a pretty decent selfie that does not look like a selfie.

Now that every other person on the globe has a phone with a camera, the world is awash in selfies. Perhaps we are a nation of narcissists. Or maybe because of technology we feel the need to document everything – and include a self-portrait in the picture. Or maybe we are just lonely and it is nice to see a familiar face at a ballgame, or at a concert, or eating a Tex-Mex combo platter.

Church can fall into cultural quagmire of selfishness too. Small-groups, Sunday School classes, and ministries can look like "selfies" that are familiar, yet lonely. Long ago disciples hid behind locked doors out of fear, but Jesus not only found his way in, but in turn opened the doors wide – "No more selfies! Get out there and love the neighbor, the stranger, and the outsider like I taught you!" (That is the Greg DeLoach Version [*GDV*] from Matthew 28:19)

In this life God created us not to live as walking "selfies" but to live in vibrant community. While the phrase "Covenant of God" sounds heavy with legalism, it really is a generous invitation to save us from ourselves so that we can live more fully with one another. Life together is not a closed community of insiders against the outsiders, but a porous way of living, relating, serving and advocating. A cursory reading of the Bible reminds us that God is particularly concerned about neighbors, outsiders, and strangers.

One of the most memorable stories Jesus told followed an exchange over the commandments. Nowadays we either recoil at the thought of debating law or we settle back in polite boredom. Jesus has a way of transforming commandments into purposeful living. Jesus taught that to love God and love one's neighbor were the two most important commandments and then tells the story of "The Good Samaritan." The story ends with a surprise resolution of the outsider doing good to the one most in need, to which Jesus asks: "Which of these…was a neighbor to the man who fell into the hands of the robbers?" The answer is obvious: "The one who showed him mercy." (Luke 10:36-37)

The commissioning is obvious too: Jesus said to him, "Go and do likewise."

May God commission you on a mission of mercy with your family, with your colleagues, and with complete strangers. May your "selfies" be filled with neighbors and acts of generosity.

Peace and love be yours this day...

Part Three: Journey of Gratitude

You search out my path and my lying down, and are acquainted with all my ways. Psalm 139:3

A Life of Gratitude

Meister Eckhart, in his contemplative and mystical work *Cloud of Unknowing*, wrote, "If the only prayer you ever say in your entire life is thank you, it will be enough."

I am discovering these days that gratitude marks most of my prayers when, especially when I am not sure what else to say. It is not that I am thankful for all events in my life. Certainly not. I am not thankful about pain or suffering, especially when it involves those whom I love the most. I am not thankful for evil in this world, or the hateful speech I hear, or the unloving acts against others.

But I am grateful to share in this life with others as we confront a world that is often broken, suffering, and wanting for love.

Father David Steindl-Rast presented a Ted-Talk and said that the one thing that unites all persons everywhere is that we all want to be happy. Some think that when you are happy you are grateful, but this monk challenges us to think again. It is not that gratitude comes from happiness, but that when we are grateful we are happy. I think he is right.

I have lived, for the most part, a happy life, but not because my moments are filled with pleasure. It is the moments when I can slow down enough to be grateful: grateful for good food, and the hands that have prepared it; grateful to see my sweet wife smile when I walk in the door in the evening; grateful for a random call from one of my sons wanting just to say hi; grateful for the arc of my life that has included so many interesting, diverse people who have taught me and teach me still. Grateful.

I am grateful too for those who listen to my own wandering thoughts behind pulpits, blogs and conference rooms. We all desire to be heard, and so I have been blessed beyond measure to be surrounded by such a great cloud of witnesses.

I am learning to mark my steps with gratitude – for breath and strength and the capacity to say, "I love you." No matter how far I walk in this world, my steps are wasted if I am not grateful.

To be grateful shapes every relationship on earth as well as in heaven.

Gratitude is prayer. Gratitude is life. Gratitude is really the only thing we can leave behind to share with others.

Friends

When I was a child, friendships came easily. All I had to do was "play nice," and just like that, friendships were formed. I remember swinging with Harold on the playground. We talked about what we wanted to be when we grew up and how we would be friends forever, maybe even live in the same neighborhood. Harold was African-American. Back then I did not know about issues of race or the divisions of class distinctions. I just knew that Harold was my friend.

But as I grew older friendships became more complicated. Cars, clothes and relationships were sources of competition. As such, my circle of friendships grew smaller. No longer was it a matter of swinging on the playground during recess. It was more of an issue of popularity, and as such friendships were like commodities to be used and traded.

Entering college, I left behind my childish ways, as well as most of my friends. It was not so much a rejection of my childhood friends as it was geography. I was 180 miles away from my hometown. When I moved to seminary it was nearly 500 miles away. Nevertheless, more than thirty years later there are many of my friends from childhood that I have not seen since the day I received my High School diploma. Harold, along with a few others, has since passed away.

College, and later seminary, brought new friends, but, as with my childhood, life's progressions like graduation, family and career would eventually leave many – most – of my friends behind in a nostalgic wake of memory.

I never learned to cultivate healthy friendships in my adult years. As a pastor, it seemed difficult to have friends, because I was always, well, a pastor to others. In seminary, I was taught the importance of having friendships *outside* the church, but that it was not recommended to make friends in the church you serve. Church members need you to be, so the lesson went, a pastor and not a friend. Twenty-eight years as a pastor I can say that is mostly true, whether I wanted it to be or not. It is hard to be both, which just left me with more loneliness.

Here I am in my 50's looking back and looking ahead and acknowledging that friendships are essential to life. Whether I regret not having more friends during the first few decades of adulthood are of less importance to me than nourishing the friendships I have today.

Today I have wonderful friends and I count it a generous grace that I share my life with them. Looking ahead my goal is not so much to make more friends, but to deepen the friendships I have. Along the way, however, I will be much less cautious about forming friendships. If others want to sit awhile in my company, then I am grateful. The need to compete, work, protect or use is a season now fading in my life.

I can never have enough friends, and I am grateful for all the ones whom I call "my friends."

> *Oh, I'm a lucky man, to count on both hands the ones I love*
> *Some folks just have one, yeah, others, they've got none.*
> (Eddie Vedder of *Pearl Jam*)

Yes, I will take care of what time is left in my life for the friendships I have. I will also be wondrously open to the new friends who may come my way. Putting away childish ways should never include friends. In this I want to be forever young.

A Lamp unto My Desk

At the tender age of 22 I had served the good folks of Unity Baptist for nearly two years. During that time, I grew a beard, got engaged, married, finished college, and prepared to move to Louisville, KY to attend seminary. This church loved me through and through, even though I was not much better behind the pulpit than when I started and had lots to learn about being a pastor. Still, they blessed me and bless me still.

My final Sunday with them came on a warm May morning. There was a covered dish luncheon following the service, so the pressure was on to keep my sermon brief. At the luncheon Amy and I were showered with affection, cards, well-wishes, and one very special gift from the church – a brass desk lamp. It was given to me with the hope that it would help me through my studies in seminary, as well as the many years ahead as a pastor.

I have lugged that lamp with me – all the way to Kentucky and back – for the last quarter of a century. As a student, it was perched on my desk in the corner of our tiny apartment, illuminating my studies even though Hebrew was still dark and mysterious. It has traveled with me to some great pastorates in Georgia including Mansfield, Chickamauga, Marietta and for the last ten years Augusta. On cold days, I place my hands over the brass shade to enjoy a little warmth. When days are short and mornings and evenings are dark, it casts a beautiful glow from my study. On any day, year-round it is usually the only source of light, besides what the windows let in.

When I look at that lamp I remember the beautiful congregation that blessed me – a church that no longer meets, because few people want to go to country churches anymore. I also think about the friends we made there who cast light into our lives.

When I look at that lamp I also experience the continued glow of friends and family I have made over the years among the churches I have served. I am so grateful for the churches and people that have enlightened my life with love and grace. Wherever I go, I am confident that I will discover what I already know, this light grows brighter and bigger because of the many people who have joined with me along my walk.

When Jesus speaks of letting our light shine I think one of the best ways we do that is through holy friendships. Genuine community casts a light that darkness cannot comprehend. Thank you, friends, for letting me walk a while in your light.

Seeing and Saying Thanks

There is so much in life that is not fully appreciated until it is a memory. Relationships come quickly to mind. When Amy and I were newlyweds we lived on a *very* meager income, rented a garage apartment that smelled of mothballs, and did not have a television for the first six months of marriage. It seems such a long time ago when we were young and clueless, and yet as I remember that first year my heart is warmed with gratitude that Amy and I said, "I do."

A few years later children forevermore changed our lives. During those early days when our boys were infants, there were (it seemed at the time) endless and exhausting midnight feedings and diapering, as well as long sleepless nights of colic. To be honest, it was just about impossible to notice and be grateful. We were just trying to hang on and get through the day and the night. Yet looking back I am grateful, even for those grueling days of early parenting.

When our children were still small and young, I would sometimes gripe about driving all over the state to visit relatives during the holidays and wonder if we should just stay home. Now many of those same relatives are no longer in this world, and I wish I could just share a sandwich and a memory.

We do not always see our gratitude until it is a reflection of the past. And then we are often rushing right past gratitude on the way to something else. Even the formal season called Thanksgiving is both brief and overshadowed by the more commercialized Black Friday and Cyber Monday of the Christmas season. Who has time for thanksgiving when there is a shiny object to buy?

To be grateful is to both see and say our thanks. Alan Culpepper writes in his fine commentary on Luke: "Gratitude may be the purest measure of one's character and spiritual condition." Of course, he is right. To be grateful shapes every relationship on earth as well as in heaven.

Here is what I have witnessed leading me to give thanks:

- My life: It is far from perfect – but mine nonetheless to enjoy and live fully within.
- My wife whom I have enjoyed for well over half of my life in marriage where we are still raising each other.
- My two boys whom I admire because they are becoming not the men I want them to be, but the men they are created to be.
- Sunrises, sunsets, and nighttime skies full of stars.
- Beautiful books written by brilliant people and for all those teachers that instilled upon me a love for reading.
- The smoke of a campfire – its smell is a sacred incense of homecoming.

I am thankful too for many whom I have shared life together in the churches I have served:

- Those delicate hands, gnarled with arthritis that grab my scruffy face in an embrace.
- The children and youth whose very presence of energy blesses me beyond words.
- The stories – not just the ones of success but even the failures and tragedies, for they too have their meaning
- And yes, for the time together sharing the struggles of faith and hope.

Since I see it, I have to say it: thank you.

I Am "Running" Out of Shoes

...Well, not really. But it seems just as soon as I am breaking in a pair of running shoes, I am already getting ready for the next pair. It seems I am hard on shoes. Over the years I have developed quite a pile of smelly, worn out shoes. Some I retire to yard work. Others are still in decent enough shape to wear casually. Still some are suitable to donate to charity. There have been one or two pairs that Amy has insisted I bury deep into the woods at an undisclosed location.

Years ago, my method of replacing running shoes was pretty simple: replace them when the soles are worn smooth to the point that you could see my socks, or when the shoe itself fell apart leaving no choice. Some "experts" (those people who are paid to sell shoes) state that if you wait that long to replace shoes you are doing harm to yourself. For a person my size (about 200 pounds, give or take a cheeseburger or two) I should replace my shoes every thirty hours of running. At this point the shoes are not particularly worn to the visible eye. There is still ample tread on the soles and aside from dirt and, well, the aroma of sweat, they are in decent shape. The reason they need to be replaced is that the shock absorption of the shoe is dangerously diminished. The shoe helps take in the pounding of a heavy guy like me and therefore allegedly saves my feet, knees and back from too much wear and tear.

I suppose there are all sorts of life analogies that can be made: the danger of wearing others out beyond repair; guests that hang around too long stink; or save your "soul" before it is too late (sorry, I could not resist!). The connection I am mulling over is how necessary we are to each other. We the community of faith surround one another to help absorb the poundings, the shocks and the day to day use that wears and tears on us.

The author of Hebrews writes: "...*let us run with perseverance the race that is set before us...*" (12:1), but this is no individualistic pursuit. Spiritual formation is a journey intended for sharing. I use the term "community of faith" about as much as I use the term "church." As a community or a church, a gathering of believers and followers exist to hold one another up, absorbing and enduring with one another the impacts, poundings, and shocks inevitably encountered in life.

Paul writes in Colossians 3:13 *"Bear with one another…"* This is family. This is community. This is Church. This is community life together.

Daddy Joe

That was what everybody called him – Daddy Joe. The name his mamma gave him was Joseph Barnes DeLoach, after his grandfather, but everybody called him Daddy Joe. He was my great-grandfather and he died when I was eight years old. He lived pretty much off the same patch of clay his grandfather settled in the 1830s and did what everyone else was doing: farming and sawmilling. His first wife died in childbirth and so along with teaching his three boys how to plow behind mules, he had to learn how to make biscuits.

Daddy Joe knew of other hard times. He would live to see his middle son die "somewhere in Germany" in 1945. A few years later he watched his house burn down to the ground destroying most all of his worldly goods including the flag that draped his son's coffin. But all that was ancient history and snatches of stories when I knew him. To me he was just a thin "old" man who kept tobacco on him most all the time and who would grin when we'd come to visit and offer some of that old, stale hard candy kept in a tin nearby. He was the family patriarch and I remembered he looked just like my grandfather, "Papa," who looked just like my daddy does today.

When Daddy Joe died my grandfather became the elder, but that too would be short-lived. He passed on when I was twelve. But I was so blessed to know these two fine men. They were a part of my daddy's upbringing more so than my own, and a bit of who I am is because of who they were. I am even more blessed that my daddy is still alive, still farming in that same general area where Pea Ridge fades into Rockville.

I am not sure what Daddy Joe would think if he knew that one of his great-grandchildren grew up to be a preacher living near "Etlanta." I suppose I have come a long way from the farmers from Eatonton, but I hope not too far. My boys would will do well if some of Daddy Joe, Papa, and daddy would be reflected in the men they grow up to become.

The fifth commandment speaks of "Honoring your father and mother" (Deuteronomy 5:16). When we remember the contributions of our ancestors we honor them. I hope that you have someone to honor in your life.

If not, find an elder and make a friend. Ask for a story or two. Although the times have changed, you may discover that struggles, perseverance, and gratitude is a timeless trail we can all share.

Whatever Happened to Generation X?

As far as demographic monikers go, we frequently read and hear about Baby Boomers (those born 1945-1964) and Millennials (1985-1994). Baby Boomers were at one time the largest demographic, but Millennials have now replaced our elders as the largest demographic in America. Advertisers, marketers and churches have spent the last several decades scrambling to reach these two sizeable generations.

Somewhere along the way a generation was labeled, but soon forgotten – Generation X (those born 1965-84). This is my generation. We are not sizeable enough to warrant the attention of marketers, or anybody else for that matter. At one time, my generation was labeled the "Slacker Generation" which is now considered ironic because Generation X statistically holds the highest education levels among all the other age groups. The Pew Research Center has described my generation as America's neglected "middle child."

Oh well, in time all generations will be forgotten. I guess my generation has a head start. We are all, in the words of the writer of Ecclesiastes, "...the dust returns to the earth as it was, and the breath returns to God who gave it." In case we still do not get it, the author adds one more line: "Vanity of vanities...all is vanity." (Ecclesiastes 12:7-8)

As a people of faith our motivation is not to "target" or favor, one generation above another. We are here, to put it simply, to love one another. It is a faith issue. It is a justice issue. It is religion at its most basic.

Here is my hope for my generation as well as all generations:

- *That every life be valued.* This includes the citizen who holds membership with the Daughters of the American Revolution as well as the immigrant trying to start over. The Native American living in poverty on a reservation and the incarcerated serving a life sentence are equally valued by

their, by our, Creator. God has imbued all human beings with the gift of being created in the Image of God. It is a good and holy gift and we should value one another accordingly.
- *That love of neighbor guide public policy and private practice.* Imagine how this world would be transformed if we took Jesus at his word when he said that the love of others is one of the two greatest commandments. It would radically change everything, which I think is the point.
- *That the highest ambition is to serve and not be served.* All generations struggle against the evil forces of privilege and entitlement. What if we actively sought to change that notion by picking up our own towels to wash the feet of others?

Just like our elected officials and policy makers of today, my generation will one day be no more. And it is the same with your generation. And so, will all other generations. The Bible reminds us: *"And the world and its desire are passing away, but those who do the will of God live forever."* (1 John 2:16)

Grace to you my brother and sister…

Send Me a Text...

According to my extensive and laborious research on the internet (and if it is on the internet, it must be true, right?) texting has been around for about 25 years. For the DeLoaches, it has only been around for ten or so years – not exactly early adopters. Love it or loathe it, texting is here to stay. It seems everybody is texting these days and they are texting everywhere: in church, in cars, in meetings, in the check-out line, and even in funerals (yep, I have witnessed this more than once).

For my children, it is the primary form of communication. For me, it often substitutes for an email. For my marriage, we will use texts as reminders, and every-so-often as a "love note."

Whenever I receive a text "out of thin air" if you will, I am most often warmed with gratitude that someone, somewhere, thought of me. It may be something silly, or provocative, or somber, but to know I was remembered and "texted" is in itself a gift. I have a friend that texts me every Sunday morning. It comes as a prayer of sorts for a sermon I am about to preach.

To be thought of, to be remembered, to call to mind...it means that we matter. Our existence matters. Our place in the world matters. What we do, or not do, matters. You matter.

"What are human beings that you are mindful of them? Yet you have made them a little lower than the angels." (Psalm 8:4,5) God calls us to mind because we matter to God. We are in a real and tangible way an idea of God.

Maybe, just maybe our very purpose in life is to remember one another. We are to move through this earth on our brief journey and remember: remember our family, our friends, and our neighbors. We are to remember the neglected, the overlooked and the ignored. We are to remember our enemies, victims and the abused. We are to remember one another.

For a brief period of time I worked with persons with developmental disabilities. During that time, I discovered that my job was mostly about remembering those who are so often forgotten, neglected or ignored. It was not only a call to remember, but an effort to bring to the minds and engage the consciousness of others that they remember too.

When you remember you then have a task, a choice to respond or ignore and forget. Either way, when you remember you then must decide what to do. What you do becomes your life.

In a small way that is why I write to you…that you may know you are remembered and loved.

Thinking of you…

What is Church?

They came bearing casseroles and cakes, paper plates and folding chairs. The tiny house in front of the dairy barn was filled with folks from all over the surrounding countryside. My grandfather died during the night, quite unexpectedly and word of it passed quickly in the farming community of Putnam County. I was 12 years old, confused and devastated, but comforted by all those older women who mothered me in the days ahead. Likewise, men wearing Liberty overalls stood out in the yard, kicking dust, and told stories that made me laugh and reminded me what a fine man my grandfather was to so many.

That is church.

I remember watching church members surround this well-loved, but now devastated middle-age lady. Her son was arrested the previous week on drug charges. I had visited the young man shortly after his arrest, held his hand while he cried out of shame and disappointment, and assured him that our love was steadfast. His family was not giving up on him and neither was I.

That is church.

One Sunday we awkwardly sang songs in a "blended" worship service – a curious hybrid of hymns, modern praise choruses, drums, guitars and pipe organ. A guy with tattoos running up his neck wearing a sleeveless t-shirt, belted out his praise right beside a demure widow who was a bit uncertain about it all, but grateful for the big crowd that Sunday. Some people groused and complained, but I still carry that image with me of the big man with tattoos beside the little elderly lady holding a hymnal together.

That is church.

A phone call was taken and in the brevity of a few words it was learned that John's only remaining relative died a couple of days ago. John is an adult with developmental disabilities and was living alone in a dilapidated trailer. He was afraid and lonely and heart-sick, living in a world that too quickly values intellect and power. Once the urgency was discovered, a minister stepped in, rallied her church to do something, and a group home was founded. John now lives safely and lovingly with friends not far from where he grew up. Oh, and John sings every Sunday in the choir.

Church can be incorrigible and narrow-minded. Church can be political and short-sighted. Church can be disappointing and frustrating. I can say this about every institution I have ever been a part of, including my very own family.

Often, I read and have conversations with people giving up on the church, leaving the church, or never being a part of the church in the first place. I understand, I really do. I have wanted to storm out from time to time too, for all of the above reasons and more. "I can just love Jesus on my own, beyond the walls," I say to no one in particular.

It is helpful to remember that Jesus was quite frustrated with his religious community too. Yet he kept going, kept worshiping alongside men and women, and kept challenging others to a higher way of knowing, living and behaving. Jesus engaged the community of faith - Pharisees and sinners; Scribes and nobodies; tax-collectors and harlots - with the unyielding hope that together, in community, it is important to love one another, love the neighbor, and love God...Together.

I need a place and a people to love and be loved; I need a place and a people to find community; I need a place and a people who will hold me accountable as we seek to live out God's purpose and mission for this world. I need a place and a people to practice the faith in community and in the world.

By God's grace we are kept in this grace…together. There is always room for more.

Our Shabby Biographies

I have a couple of special places at home designated for reading. In the early morning (before daylight) I sit in my recliner in the living room. Beside my chair is an "end table" which was originally an old chamber pot bench (complete with chamber pot). On that small bench is where I stack my books. My other spot is on my back porch. I have been known to sit out there in the dead of winter - gloves, heavy coat and all - deep in a good read.

This year, for no particular reason, I have read several biographies and memoirs. Biographies are not necessarily my favorite genre, but one well written is worth the time. From Genghis Kahn to Johnny Cash, people are generally interesting if you pay attention to their story, and everybody has a story.

At the risk of sounding narcissistic, sometimes I wonder what an author might write about my life. "A thoughtful soul; quick to laugh at sophomoric things; and has a fondness for strange antiques." No doubt my biographer would pour over all my writings, including articles like this one. From such research, it could be said of me, "Grammatically clumsy, but passionate in convictions and winsome with nostalgia." Of course, biographers have to get into the family background and here again I am not wanting for material. "An eclectic upbringing; surrounded by hard-working farmers on the rocky piedmont soil of middle Georgia."

A good biography usually shows the complexity of its subject. No one person is "all good" (not even Johnny Cash) or "all bad" (same with Genghis Khan). People are complicated, often at odds within themselves, and at times duplicitous with convictions.

What would your biography say?

We all have shabbiness in our story. Mistakes, missteps, and outright embarrassments litter our personal narratives.

The poetry of faith reminds us that redemption is not one-time, but on-going. John Claypool would conclude worship with the words,

"You are being redeemed" and that is true. Our biographies are always changing, day by day, moment by moment. There are highlights and accomplishments we hope will always be remembered. And there are set-backs and failures we pray will soon be forgotten.

Your story is important and I hope you find strength to share it. The old-fashioned word for this is testimony, which is just another way of saying share.

Share your story with others. Your funny memories as well as your times of failures are stories that can strengthen and comfort others. In sharing with others, you build connections and from connections you build trust and from trust come an abundance of generative beginnings.

As you go forth in this day, remember that you are writing your biography of your "one wild and precious life" (Mary Oliver).

May your story speak of great adventures, even in the mundane chores.

May your story tell of great grace, even when you experience great disappointments.

May your story share God's fidelity, even when your strength fails you.

Recall Notice

One morning I had what can delicately be described as a "wardrobe malfunction." It was not nearly as sensational as the infamous episode many years ago during the half-time of the Super Bowl, but it was nevertheless inconvenient. The right arm (or is it a leg?) of my eye glasses fell off, and despite all my efforts it would not reassemble. In ten minutes I was to preach, and unless something changed I would be preaching in the dark. Actually, it would be more like preaching in the blur. I trotted in a stumbling, woozy, nearsighted kind of way to my Jeep, which was inconveniently parked on the far side of the parking lot, to retrieve an old pair of glasses that would see me through the day (get the pun?). By the time I returned to the worship service in progress it was five minutes before the sermon and I was rumpled, ruffled and not a little bit sweaty. I imagine you think that preachers are in a blissful state of prayer and union with God right before the sermon, but on that particular day I was just trying to survive.

That afternoon with some *crazy glue* I temporarily repaired my glasses and was able to enjoy the Sunday paper without much squinting. The following week I returned to the optical store to have my glasses repaired and it was there I learned that there was a recall notice on my glasses – a recall! I have been wearing glasses since I was seven and have never once had a pair that was later recalled. Whoever heard of such? Was there concern that the airbags would not deploy properly or that the brakes might fail?

Not only could my glasses not be repaired, I had to now pick out a new set of frames and begin again the break-in period of a new pair of glasses. The task of trying on different frames and trusting someone else's opinion as to whether they look good on me or not is a chore for me. The problem is simple: I cannot tell what the frames look like on my face because, you guessed it, I cannot see clearly without my glasses!

Paul's words take on a new meaning for me: "For now we see through a glass, dimly…" (1 Corinthians 13:12, KJV with a minor Greg DeLoach translation).

Such is life for all of us. Our view and perspective, even at its best, is still incomplete and partial. Thanks be to God for the words and lives of others that help us in our sight, like a trusty pair of glasses. Scripture, tradition, community and friendship help us stumble through this world. Indeed, *for now see through a glass dimly*… But in time, in God's generous time, "…then we will see face to face. Now I know only in part; then I will know fully, even as I have been fully known."

Grateful to look alongside you, making our way through this world and enjoying the sites…

Living Up to the Smile

There is a park alongside a river that is a convenient place for me to stop on the way home from work. While traffic hums by, there are trails winding through patches of woods, greenspace and the river itself that makes it ideal for jogging (or in my case lumbering). Just the other day as I was huffing and puffing and wondering if I was burning enough calories for a well-deserved desert, I noticed that most everyone I met along the trail was smiling at me. Some smiles are suspicious; other smiles have a hint of ridicule. But these smiles seemed genuine, happy. "Gee, there sure are a lot of nice people around here." Everyone knows that joggers usually do not smile.

And then it occurred to me: I was wearing my "smiley" shirt, but not just any smiley shirt. This shirt had the mud-splattered smiley face inspired by the fictionalized account from the movie "Forrest Gump." They are smiling at me, but more specifically they are smiling at my shirt. I attempted to live up to my good-natured shirt and smile back!

Living up to the smile. Sometimes smiles are fake, and most of us know one when we see one. Sometimes smiles are just a feeble attempt to cover up melancholy. I never like it when someone tells me, "Smile!" especially when I just do not feel like smiling.

Yet there are times when I think we are far too guarded with our smiles, as if a smile makes us vulnerable or appear weak or indolent. It is true that I sometimes smile a bit too enthusiastically for photos, but more often than I want to admit my face reflects selfish distractions.

I love to be around smiles that come freely and generously. I love to see smiles because something is silly and it is okay to enjoy the moment. I love it when someone greets me with a smile, simply because they are happy to see me.

In a world deafened by traffic noises, acerbic political discourse, and mean-spirited exchanges, we need more smiles of kindness. Paul writes: *Be kind and compassionate to one another* (Ephesians 4:32) and more simply, *Love is kind* (1 Corinthians 13). There is just too much meanness in the world, and worse, too many of us who tolerate it, as if we endorse such surliness, by calling it "righteous indignation."

Our face often publicizes what is going on in our hearts.

May God grace you with something that will bring a smile to your face.

May you find time to reflect on loved ones and let your smile show.

May you, for no particular reason, smile at someone else and by doing so, open up a window of kindness to another.

Old Notebooks

Since 1985 I have kept notebooks and journals to record personal thoughts, make notes, list needs to be remembered in prayer, and offer reflections on everything from the weather to a new idea picked up in a book. For the better part of a decade I have also kept a "garden journal" where I jot observations of the goings and comings of my back yard. In that notebook, I scribble down notations of how things are growing (or not), what is blooming and when, and what mammals, birds or reptiles are on the move. There is another journal I keep that was given to me when I graduated from seminary. It is a record book of baptisms, marriages and funerals.

For no particular reason, I will occasionally take one of my old notebooks from the shelf and read snatches from my past. Some inclusions are pithy and simplistic and quite frankly embarrassing to read. I am thinking to myself, "I cannot believe I wrote that…thought that…how *naïve!*" Yet it is part of my past. Some entries list the names of great people whom I heard preach, teach or lecture; many of which have returned to the earth from which they were created. My personal journals include thoughts and struggles as well as joys and hopes. My old notebooks and journals are simple reminders of where I have been – good and bad, memorable and forgettable. In the end, they are just pieces of paper that will one day come to nothing.

No doubt you are familiar with the saying, "Life is an open book," and I suppose in many ways this is true. Each waking moment is its own blank page waiting for our mark as well as the marks left by others. What I am discovering is that what will remain is not what I record on paper, but the impression I leave on others. I hope what lives on will be the love I have for my wife and my boys and my family, and not my failures, shortcomings and mistakes. I also hope to leave behind a legacy of love for others – my neighbor, the stranger, and even my enemies.

Life is an open book, and I am writing the pages. One day God will write the ending and the final word will be grace. God's one word will be the only word that really matters. May it be the word found throughout my pages – and yours too.

In your book were written all the days that were formed for me... (Psalm 139:16)

Kept in the firm grip of grace...

Hugging Trees and Thanking God

God saw everything that he had made, and indeed, it was very good. (Genesis 1:31)

Do you remember when you first discovered that the world, the earth is a beautiful place? Perhaps you were on a family vacation and you were gripped by exploding autumn colors in the Great Smoky Mountains. Or you hiked with your parents to a waterfall and for the first time were overwhelmed as the mist enfolded you and the water thundered down. When was it that you discovered the beauty of creation? Staring at Orion galloping across the evening sky or peering through the telescope to see the craters of the moon?

Early in college I took an interest in ecology and the environment and found myself accused of being a tree-hugger. Well I must confess I am. I love trees. Many mornings you might see me walking around this campus admiring the stately live oaks, redbuds, and Japanese Maples that mark our grounds. With great affection, I remember the first tree I fell in love with when I was a boy. It was a giant sycamore that to this day still looms over a creek that runs through the pasture bottoms where the dairy cows graze before the afternoon milking. When we were small children my daddy and grandparents would take us to that spot to play in the sand alongside that sycamore whose roots reached beneath the creek itself while the massive limbs shaded us from the scorching summer sun.

During early spring, trees around us are shaking off winter's sleep and opening up delicate new leaves for the year. Years ago, I dug up a water-oak sapling growing in the pasture beside my home place and transplanted it to the front yard of the pastorium of Mansfield Baptist Church, where we had just moved from Louisville, KY. That was twenty-five years ago. Today that sapling is a large oak, giving shade to different occupants who know nothing about the trees origins.

I wonder what other gifts I am leaving behind that will give shade to the weary and inspiration to the seeker? Will it be words spoken or written? Will it be laughter or integrity or a hopeful attitude? What gifts will live on when I am gone? Surely, hopefully, prayerfully it will be something more than just "stuff." What about you?

Gifts that live on are part of the larger narrative of Eastertide. Easter is not simply a celebration of a particular Sunday once a year. The Easter crowd is glorious to see, but surely this is not just once a year. Liturgists remind us that Easter is a season that carries us into the year. Even now God is offering new life to all who are willing to receive it. There are more gifts to behold and accept and so life can begin anew today, right now. And not only are there gifts of grace that are waiting for you, you too have the chance to bless, to care, to love, and to show mercy. These are the gifts that truly live on when we are no more on this earth.

The silence of Lenten winter is broken by the Alleluia of the One who makes all things new. May this be for you a promise realized, in season and out.

Shaded by peace…

If There Was One Word…

There are many good and necessary words in my theological vocabulary. The word "love" goes without saying, but goodness knows it needs to be said nowadays. Speaking of goodness, I would add good. Mercy, justice, and steadfast are all important words. Sin too, and with it forgiveness. As I reflect over a theological vocabulary, there are many, many words that come to mind. What words would you add?

If there was only one word to sum up the entirety of my own working theology, it would be this – *grace*. I am not sure when this word became THE word for me, but somewhere along the path it laid claim to my loyalties. While there is no candle on the Advent wreath dedicated to grace, there ought to be and we ought to light it daily.

Grace means gift. It is a gift freely given that comes without merit or works. All of my life I have been blessed with gifts that I did not deserve, nor ask for. I was born in a part of the world that gave me privileges and opportunities. My father and grandparents loved and provided for me; church nurtured me; and teachers who…well, they tried their best! All of my life I have been blessed with gifts that I did not deserve, but gratefully received.

This is not to say that all of my life has been idyllic or charmed. At a young age, my parents divorced. Growing up on the family dairy farm meant that much of the time we had very little in the way of luxuries compared to my friends. Neither was their much in the way of time to just simply play. My grandfather died unexpectedly and young (59). I watched my mother-in-law suffer with Alzheimer's before passing away far too young.

It is what I have been given and not what I do not have that I choose to call Grace. Too often, I am afraid, I see what I have missed, or what I am denied, and find it tempting to succumb to resentment or worse, a sense of entitlement.

Do you know God's grace? The kind of grace that reaches deep into your life in a way that you know all of life is a gift; a wondrous, marvelous, and sometimes troubling gift. One of my favorite rock bands, U2, sings about grace in song by the same title:

> *Because grace makes beauty*
> *Out of ugly things*
>
> *Grace finds beauty*
> *In everything*
>
> *Grace finds goodness*
> *In everything*

One of the big graces I have experienced throughout my adult life is the grace in sharing my life with others. And when you have been given a gift, a grace, the appropriate response is to say, "thank you."

Thank you for being a part of my life...

Broken Things...

One Sunday morning I was making my routine rounds during the Sunday School hour. It is one of my favorite parts of the day as I stick my head in the classes of the young and the old to say, "good morning," grip and grin, and maybe snag a pastry (any pastry will do) on the way out. Please do not worry about the last part, the part about the pastries, because I limit myself to only three or four; maybe five if it is homemade. Anyway, on this day I was hustling out of the preschool building in kind of a hurry because, as we all know, doughnuts are hard to come by there, In my haste my beloved coffee cup – the one made by a gifted local potter – slipped from my hand and broke in three distinct pieces. Ugh. I carried the remains back to my office, searched for some glue, but in vain gave up and left the cup on an unsuspecting assistant's desk (whom I thought might have glue).

Two days later my cup was back on my desk, mended and restored. It was almost as good as new, except for the mended cracks. I found out later one of the custodians saw it, recognized it was my cup, and repaired it.

Some broken things can be mended. Some not. I remember late one summer hearing on the news of the death of comedian and actor Robin Williams. He was a broken man who just could not get mended. I am still sad for the loss of this life.

Every day we are moving around and alongside broken things and broken people. Some things you see: a wheelchair, a cane, a cast, a band-aide – symbols of broken bodies. Some things, perhaps most things, you do not see, because they are buried deep beneath the effortful facades and barriers that come by way of suppression and shame. Only the bearers of such brokenness see, but even then, it can be too confusing, too overwhelming, to really see, let alone understand.

Mystics sometimes call this the dark night of the soul, but when one is broken on the inside or the outside it is often not just a night, but a season and maybe even a life clouded and dimmed by chaos. Why is it that some whose things are not observably broken smash upon the brittle lives of others? Or perhaps even more indicting, ignore and neglect by a failure of love and compassion? Why do some condescend with quick fixes, simplistic answers, and pithy responses adorned with pious clichés?

The community of believers is also a communion of brokenness. As broken bread is held up as a sacrament of Christ's own brokenness, we too are drawn into this communion with our scarred bodies and brittle minds and failing spirits.

I am so grateful for the one who took my little coffee cup and mended it just for me. I am grateful too for the community of believers that gathers together with our nicks, scars, chips, and cracks to find wholeness in togetherness. And I am grateful for the One who entered our brokenness and became broken that we all may be made eternally whole.

[We] need to hear that still small voice saying, 'I love you whether you are important or not, whether you are a failure or not, whether you have money or not, whether you are handsome or not. (Henri Nouwen, "The Road to Daybreak", p. 194)

Going Places

Years ago, when my boys were, well boys, we were all sitting together as a family about to have supper. It was Aaron's turn to ask the blessing, which was also a mixed blessing. Sometimes this six-year-old would feel exceptionally pious and righteous and was compelled to pray for all the world – one name at a time. Other times he just wanted to get on with the business of eating (yeah, that's my son). Following what I thought was an impressive blessing, I turned to him and said, "Gee Aaron that was a really beautiful prayer. You are going to make a great pastor one day." "No daddy," he replied, "I am not going to be a pastor." Amy grinned, the dog looked up and curiosity got the better of me. "Why not?" I implored, "It's great work being a pastor." Aaron responded in a rather condescending tone, "Daddy, I don't want to be a pastor, *I am going places*."

Ouch. Up until that point I had always looked at my calling as taking me to great places. I have lived in such extravagant places like Rome (GA not Italy), the Philippines, Louisville, Mansfield, Chickamauga and at that time just a few miles from "the Big Chicken." Where exactly did my youngest son plan to go?

"Going places" is a worthy pursuit, however, and I am proud that in whatever way Aaron interpreted that, he saw it as important. It behooves us to ask of ourselves, "where am I going?" Living life thoughtfully and abundantly is how I understand "going places." Seizing both joy and meaning from the everyday to the extraordinary is a holy endeavor. "*Finally, beloved, whatever is true, whatever is honorable, whatever is just, whatever is pure, whatever is pleasing, whatever is commendable, if there is any excellence and if there is anything worthy of praise, think about these things.*" (NRS Philippians 4:8)

Well don't just sit there – get going with the business of life and go places!

Seeing the World Through My Dog's Nose

In nearly three decades of marriage we have shared life with a number of animals (besides our children). There was "Bro" the hamster, fondly remembered for his...well, come to think of it, I don't really remember much about him. When he passed on from this world, my sons held a funeral for him, including a stirring harmonica solo of "Amazing Grace." For many years we kept an aquarium full of cichlids (cousins of piranhas, but smaller and with less teeth). I am not sure what happened to them, but I think algae was involved. We briefly owned a cat that I named after one of my favorite theologians, "Jurgen," which sounds a lot better than Jurgen's last name, "Moltmann." She was a stray and unfortunately brought in stray parasites that were not welcomed in our home.

We have had three dogs. The first one was a sweet beagle named "Molly." She was not long for this world, so I will not go into it for this article. "Samson" was our beloved yellow lab for 12 years. When he died our hearts were so broken we could not think of having another dog for another 7 years. Finally, this past summer, we saw a little pup at a rescue shelter and our hearts were moved. "Annie" has been part of the family ever since.

Taking Annie out for walks can be a frustrating undertaking if what you want to do is actually walk. The walks are more like high speed sprints, interspersed with languid pauses so she can smell – I mean thoroughly smell – whatever is on the ground, in the air, along the sidewalk, etc. Tugging at the leash; calling her away; bribing her with treats; will not sway this canine daughter from her task of deep thinking through her nose.

A dog experiences the world primarily through smell. Sure, many have great hearing and some breeds have remarkable eyesight, but it is with the nose where the action is. According to NOVA, a dog "possess up to 300 million olfactory receptors in their noses, compared to about six million in us. And the part of a dog's brain that is devoted to analyzing smells is, proportionally speaking, 40 times greater than ours." If our coffee has a teaspoon of sugar added to it, so claims the article, a dog could detect a teaspoon of sugar in two Olympic-sized pools worth.

I am learning…oh so haltingly…to appreciate the world through my dog's nose. I know that very image is a silly one, but think about it (or to stay on point, smell on it). We tend to view others through our own exclusive perspective. That means we bring our experiences, our biases, our knowledge, and our culture to bear on our understanding. As such, we do not understand and therefore we are at risk of reacting fearfully and uncharitably. But there is always more to the story; more to see, hear, and, yes, smell.

Thinking through my dog's nose is a reminder to me the importance of seeking an understanding of another; to sit in their space; to see through their experiences; and by doing so enlarge my own. The word compassion literally means to have passion with another; to join in their world which will make your own world richer.

The great stories of Jesus are full of such examples. He met the woman at the well; he walked alongside lepers and beggars; he stood in the pool of a man born blind; he held the hand of a daughter and gave her life back. Maybe the real miracle is that Jesus – God Incarnate – chose to share space with others and share in life together.

It is interesting that you do not read of Jesus demanding others to meet him where he was. Even when he invited the men to put down their nets and follow him, he first met them at the shores where they were plying their trade. Afterwards, they all crashed a party at a sinner's home.

Seeing the world through my dog's nose can be an invitation to experience every encounter with another as an opportunity for a holy meeting – so I don't want to be blind to that!

Part Four: Wandering with Mystery

"We are born to wander through a chaos field. And yet we do not become hopelessly lost, because each walker who comes before us leaves behind a trace for us to follow."

— Robert Moor

A Place to Call Home

A place to call home – we all seek such a place. Over the years Amy and I have been pretty good at nesting for ourselves places to call home - even when we knew our stay would be temporary. Our first "home" was a tiny garage apartment in Rome, Georgia. Whenever our landlady would crank her '72 Buick the roar of the motor would shake books off of our shelves. Our next home was our seminary apartment. It was an efficiency unit, which meant that you could place your hand in every room in the apartment while seated at the kitchen table. We loved our apartments and they were as much a home to us as if they were the finest castles of the world.

Since our time in seminary, we have lived in two very fine parsonages that we also called home. In fact, one of them was the largest home we have ever lived in and more than likely ever will. We have lived in temporary homes while waiting to buy more "permanent" homes and once we lived in a rental home before moving to a new city. As of this writing, we live in a comparatively small home on a small lot surrounded by a diversity of neighbors ranging in age from "fresh out of college," to "long put out to pasture." We are the empty nesters in the middle and could not be happier with our place to call home.

Home is much more than a slice of real estate or a postal address. It is as much a residence of the spirit and province of the consciousness. Do you remember when Jesus reminded his disciples, "... do not be anxious about your life, what you shall eat or what you shall drink, nor about your body, what you shall put on. Is not life more than food, and the body more than clothing?" (Matthew 6:25) These words may not mean much to those of us who stay air-conditioned in the summer and centrally heated in the winter, but what about those families who lose their homes to earthquakes, floods, or other natural disasters?

If nothing else calamities are brusque reminders of the temporal natures of our houses. To be truly home, however, has a lasting permanence. For ancient Israel, to be home was not necessarily to be in a certain geographic region but to be with God. All of us will spend the rest of our lives searching for and making homes. Please do not confuse them with bricks and mortar. These will one day come to nothing. Our home is with God and this may take us to the far corners of the globe or simple down the shaded street.

Rev. Barbara Brown Taylor writes, *we can serve the God who feeds and clothes and shelters by doing some of that ourselves, but always with the knowledge that it is God who provides -no - who is our true and only home, in whose household there is plenty - for the birds of the air, for the lilies of the field, and for every one of us.*

Disabling an Omnipotent God

Through the years, with churches and a non-profit, my work with the developmentally disabled leads me to periodically reflect on what disabilities have to say about God and humanity.

When we speak of God we often think in categories of "omni," as in "omnipotent" (all-powerful); "omniscient" (all-knowing); or "omnipresent" (all-present).

Have you ever thought of God as disabled? What comes to your mind when you hear the word, "Disabled?" Some synonyms for this word include incapacitated, restricted, immobilized, hindered. Hardly words appropriate for the Lord of the Universe.

Again, I ask, have you ever thought of God as disabled?

The Bible does. In Isaiah, we read:

he had no form or majesty that we should look at him,
 nothing in his appearance that we should desire him.
³ He was despised and rejected by others;
 a man of suffering[a] and acquainted with infirmity;
and as one from whom others hide their faces[b]
 he was despised, and we held him of no account. (53:2b-3)

But the text that really grabs me by the collar and shakes me is the ancient hymn Paul quotes in Philippians chapter 2:

Let the same mind be in you that was[a] in Christ Jesus,
⁶ who, though he was in the form of God,
 did not regard equality with God
 as something to be exploited,
⁷ but emptied himself,
 taking the form of a slave,
 being born in human likeness.
And being found in human form,
⁸ he humbled himself
 and became obedient to the point of death—
 even death on a cross. (5-8)

There it is in black and white and Helvetica type: the disabled God.

And even in the resurrection, we have reminders of God's sacred condescending to us. "Jesus was resurrected," as theologian Roberta Bondi once wrote, "scars and all."

In this world, we madly scramble towards perfection and idolize those we think are perfect. Botox promises perfect cheeks; contacts will give us perfect eye color; wealth managers guide us towards perfect retirements; and though none of us will make it, we can watch our Olympians achieve perfection in the swimming pool, the track and the balance beam.

Who has room in their mind for handicaps and limitations? It should come as no mystery then how tragic and cosmically cruel it can feel when we slam face-first into our limitations. There is the depression that clouds the heart with doubt and despair; the heart murmur suggesting all is not well; the trick knee that no longer allows you to run the bases for the softball team; or the mysterious lump that shows up in a radiology report.

Each year I turn a year older, and by successfully surviving I receive a number assigned to my age. It serves as a symbolic marker that not only am I no longer a vibrant youth, I will no longer be as strong, as handsome, as smart, as talented, as was my potential a short decade ago.

And that is okay.

I am loved by a disabled God, dwelling in a disabled world, and somehow, in the sacred mystery of it all, I am enabled by this to live out my life. So are you, thanks be to God, who was resurrected, wounds and all.

Bro is No Mo

For a few brief years we housed a *Phodopus*, more commonly known as a "dwarf hamster," or as Amy called it, a rat. Aaron just called him "Bro." Bro was his idea, which probably comes as no surprise. He bought this nocturnal rodent with money he was supposed to use for school lunches. Speaking of nocturnal, Bro loved to exercise on his wheel starting at, say, 10 PM and remained devoted to his exercise regime until about 5 or 6 AM. Each night I was lulled into sleep with the turns of the rat wheel and each morning it was still spinning to greet me for the day as I began my own rat race.

Then it happened. A day or so passed and I did not hear the wheel turn. Ah, a peaceful evening. By the next night I suggested to Aaron that it was quiet, unusually so, from Bro's abode. Upon further inspection, we both discovered that "Bro was no mo." Since there seemed to be an unwritten but mutually assumed advanced directive that discouraged "extraordinary life-saving measures," both boys (by now Clark was involved in the grieving process) commenced with funeral proceedings. This included the obligatory digging of the grave, which did not take long, and preparing the headstone accompanied by selections from the soundtrack "O Brother Where Art Thou." Years later when we sold the house we left the headstone intact, dutifully noting the understated and brief life of Bro, a rodent of rodents.

Perhaps Bro's untimely passing – although I have no idea of the lifespan of a hamster – has something to say for the rest of us. We walk this earth gently and we hold onto things loosely – even rodents (or maybe especially rodents). In the words of the Preacher of Ecclesiastes, *"To everything there is a season, and a time to every purpose under the heaven…"* (KJV 3:1) Seasons come and go, like barren trees starting to bud, or autumn air marked by early morning chill.

Some changes are welcome, but many changes leave us anxious and unmoored. When facing change sometimes we grieve over our loss, what use to be but is no more. Perhaps at work you find that there are additional responsibilities, or a new supervisor, or a change in business. Maybe you are reading this at home and you see your children growing up and out, while your parents are growing old and frail. Not sure of what is ahead, it is tempting to look back nostalgically and think it was much better back then.

And then there are those times we pursue change thinking that something else is better. In the 1920s there was a folk song called *The Big Rock Candy Mountain*, (it is one of the songs on the soundtrack "O Brother Where Art Thou," but I digress). Some sing in that wishful hope that a big rock candy mountain is just around the bend and say: *when my babies can walk…when they go to school…when they graduate…when I get promoted…when I retire…when these changes take place everything will be better.* Meanwhile, discontent stirs and change unfurls its surprises.

To be content is to trust that God will provide the security and strength to meet the change you are facing. Listen to Paul the Apostle's words to the church in Philippi:

> …for I have learned to be content with whatever I have…I know what it is to have little, and I know what it is to have plenty. In any and all circumstances I have learned the secret of being well-fed and of going hungry, of having plenty and of being in need. I can do all things through him who strengthens me. (4:11-13)

We walk this earth gently and we hold all things loosely and in all and through all of life's changes God sojourns with us bringing about Holy transformation.

Being transformed with you.

Dark Energy

…that sounds so mysterious, doesn't it? Well, it is indeed mysterious. Recently I was listening to a podcast where a physicist was interviewed about his ideas of the "consciousness of contemplation" – or something like that! He kept referring to "dark energy." "What is dark energy?" I asked out loud to no one in particular, especially since I was riding in my car by myself. Finally, the physicist speaking in the broadcast answered my question. Dark energy is the most popular way to explain recent observations and experiments that the universe appears to be expanding at an accelerating rate. It is thought that it accounts for 74% of the total mass-energy of the universe. (Thank you, Wikipedia, for convenient statistics that I will just have to trust are accurate)

The very thought that there is energy out there – which cannot fully be explained, let alone defined – that accounts for most of the energy in the known universe is enough to make one's neurons pop. A few hundred years ago it was thought that the earth was the center of the universe. Now we know that not only is the earth not the center of the universe, but it is not even the center of the solar system in this galaxy. We are just a suburb spinning on the relative margins. Furthermore, our galaxy, according to some astronomers, is just one of hundreds of billions of galaxies. Our solar system is just one among billions and billions of other galaxies, known and unknown.

The very thought alone draws me into a sense of Biblical awe and reverence. Long before telescopes and microscopes the Psalmist thought as much. In Psalm 8 David wrote (and no doubt sung) "When I look at your heavens, the work of your fingers, the moon and the stars that you have established; what are human beings that you are mindful of them, mortals that you care for them?" Again, in Psalm 19 we read: "The heavens are telling the glory of God; and the firmament proclaims his handiwork. Day to day pours forth speech, and night to night declares knowledge."

There is so much we do not know. Ralph Waldo Emerson wrote: "Knowledge is knowing that we cannot know." This is not an excuse for ignorance mind you; just a humble reminder that life is vast and ultimately incomprehensible. We do not know about the future, much less our present. We do not know about how it will all work out with our families, our finances, our health and so on. There is only so much telescopes and microscopes can tell us. The rest is mystery…holy, sacred mystery.

It is not what we know that validates our faith. It is who we know that graces us with peace. Both knowledge and ignorance can shackle us to fear, and its sibling anxiety. To rest in the "Name above all names" can set us free.

To the one struggling to find a job…*may the peace of Christ hold you.*

To the one whose family is a disaster…*may the presence of God sustain you.*

To the one cowed by the "dark cloud" of anxiety…*may the Spirit fill you.*

To all of us propelled forward in this expanding universe headed into an uncertain future, *may we look up and experience the Word that calls forth creation to live, to love, and to hope.*

In Jesus name.

Time is...

"Time is but the stream I go a-fishing in. I drink at it; but while I drink I see the sandy bottom and detect how shallow it is. Its thin current slides away, but eternity remains."

— Henry David Thoreau, *Walden*

On a morning that radiated summer heat, several of us gently gathered into the sanctuary to sit awhile with our thoughts, remembering and giving thanks for a college professor whom we all loved. For some he was a colleague and friend, who could be found coaxing a fire at a campsite, or paddling his canoe along a river, or mulling over an article just published. For others, including me, he was a teacher and mentor. His lectures were laced with snatches of German, quotes from Thoreau, and musings on God. Gentle, but solid, he changed the lives of many, including my own, by reminding us that life was too beautiful to live carelessly; too brief to live without passion; too precious to live without hope.

Looking around that morning there were fellow classmates now thirty years older and thirty years grayer, as well as former professors long retired from their lecterns. It was a tender time with the air filled with eulogies (good words) spoken and unspoken. It was a blessed moment in time where tears were mixed with gratitude.

Just a few days later I was back in Northwest Georgia visiting dear friends from my first pastorate – Unity Baptist Church. Quite a few years ago they invested in me when I was toddling 21-year-old, headstrong and full of answers no one was asking. Still these members believed in me and I came to believe in them. The church building is a charming, wood-framed structure perched on a hill surrounded by hayfields and patches of maples, oaks, and hickories. Just a few years ago the remaining membership decided to close the doors of the building for good and find new places to "go to church." No one, after all, goes to country churches anymore. The children have grown up and gone away.

Yet they are still very much the church. That night I sat with these good people around a member's pool and caught up with the couples

I married, and in the ensuing years the births of their children. Someone said: "The little ones we all remember running around and enjoying the pool are now the parents of the little ones running around and enjoying the pool."

So quickly time slips by, like Thoreau's stream. What a gift it is to look around and give thanks for the life we have lived, the ones we have loved, and those that stand with us in the flow of eternity.

I know that there is nothing better for them than to rejoice and to do good in one's lifetime; moreover, that everyone who eats and drinks sees good in all their labor- - it is the gift of God. (Ecclesiastes 3:12-13)

When the Earth Falls Away

It happens, doesn't it? You walk on this earth long enough and there will be times when what you have stood upon, depended upon, slips out from under your feet.

Some years back I answered a call from my stepmother, who, in a rather shaken voice, asked me to come home. Earlier in the day my dad was out on the tractor cutting the pastures along the creek-bottoms. Think of it as cutting your lawn, but over a much larger space, with taller grass, using heavy equipment. While going about this routine task that he has done for years, all of a sudden and without warning, the bank alongside the creek gave way and down tumbled my dad, tractor and all. Thankfully he was okay – bruised and shaken, but otherwise just fine. It was an accident that could not be prevented and it happened as suddenly and surprisingly as the earth simply disappearing.

There are times in every life when the earth just falls away beneath our feet. It can come as an accident out of nowhere that disrupts our complacency. Sometimes a nagging anxiety of failure shakes our sense of grounding. The earth can disappear whenever we experience a disappointment or a breach of trust.

How have you experienced the ground from which you stand upon give way? A demotion? A bad grade? An illness? A death? What gets you back on solid ground? For my dad, it was my brother and nephew who were "first responders." Lifting him out of the cab of the tractor from the muddy waters of the creek and onto the solid ground of the pastures restored his sure – but shaken – footing.

We all need someone who will reach into the darkness, into the calamity, into our fears to give us a steady hand of assurance and stability. The joy of belonging in friendship and family is the peace of knowing we can depend on one another; that someone will be there with the earth gives way.

It is also a way of practicing our faith together. We need each other to shore up our doubts and discouragements and to bolster our hopes. In our confessions, we preach and teach about Christ, the Solid Rock, but as important as teaching is the living and sharing. Through the years I am grateful to church members, teachers, professors, preachers, friends and family who step into my life when the earth gives way.

God is our refuge and strength, an ever-present help in trouble.
Therefore, we will not fear, though the earth give way and the mountains fall into the heart of the sea…
(Psalm 46:1-2)

Silence Can be Deafening

Silence can be deafening, especially when you are anxiously waiting to hear from someone: a call, an email, a text – anything to provide a bit of hope or assurance that all is well and all will be well. If you have been on the receiving end of a pathology report you know all too well what it feels like to wait in silence while your misery commandeers your imagination. There is the awkward silence between a couple nursing hurtful remarks. Or the silence waiting to hear about a decision from a job interview. Silence can be deafening.

We have been there with God too: waiting for a simple word, a movement, or at least a glance to reassure our fears and our anxieties.

In the early chapters of the hefty scroll of Exodus we read of Israel anguished plight of Egyptian enslavement while God is mostly passive and silent. Meanwhile we read on of kingly insecurities that lead to murderous conclusions. A baby of no particular merit is saved and given the name "Moses," which means, in part, to deliver. This happens because three women notice and do something about what they see. The baby grows up and makes some mistakes of his own, and flees the scene in exile and fear. Thus far in the story God is nowhere to be found in the first few chapters.

So the people of God cry out. It sounds a lot like Job, another character from our Bible, who is remembered as the embodiment of suffering the indignity of God's silence and apparent absence.

We need to stop right there and linger for a moment or two around the phrase *absence of God*. It seems disloyal to say it, let alone think it. It has an air of apostasy to it. Yet it is a valid expression in the Hebrew tradition. Listen to this one Psalm to get an idea of a cry of absence:

How long, O LORD? Will you forget me forever?
How long will you hide your face from me?
2 How long must I bear pain in my soul,
and have sorrow in my heart all day long?
How long shall my enemy be exalted over me?
(Psalm 13:1-2)

And this is certainly not an "Old Testament thing." We remember dark Gethsemane and the anguished prayer of Jesus asking to have the cup removed. Disciples were sleeping and God was staying quiet. There was also his disturbing cry from the cross that exclaimed God's forsakenness. Roman soldiers taunted and the bystanders jeered, while clouds gathered and the earth itself grew quiet with impending death.

Have those words every spoken for you? I realize most of us enjoy the peace and prosperity of Western civilization and have a comparatively luxurious lifestyle compared to most of the world. We are not wallowing in the poverty of Haiti or in the tyranny of Burma. No, we may not hear texts like these in the same way as oppressed people. It begs of us to ponder who are the voices of those in the world today who cry out from their suffering, injustice, oppression? They fill our prisons and our food banks. They blanket our video screens with images of sickness, hunger, and war. They are the Christians suffering in Iraq; the Buddhists beaten down in Myanmar; the Jews and the Palestinians dodging mortar fire and suicide bombers. They are the poor in Appalachia and in Detroit.

Hope is the confession that it doesn't have to stay that way. Stories in the scripture remind us that a theology that is merely passive where one is to politely wait on God and leave it to God is not the only way. Israel cries out and groans and moans…And God hears… "God heard their groaning, and God remembered his covenant with Abraham, Isaac, and Jacob….God looked upon … and God took notice …" (Exodus 2:24-25)

These old, old stories are still unfolding today in your life and mine; in communities of faith and beyond. What and who around you need to be noticed? How will God respond in you, through you, with you and beyond you?

That is our mission because it is God's mission – *The Missio Dei*; the work of God.

The Last First

It is now a ritual that on the first day of school, parents snap pictures of their children and before the kids have boarded the bus, their images are posted on Facebook. For some it is their first year and for others it is their last year. With everyone in back to school mode I get a little bit sentimental. We are no longer shopping for school supplies or anguishing over which teachers will instruct our boys (and of course the teachers were anguishing too!) and shopping for school clothes is someone else's headache. The school bus doesn't stop here anymore and so as the big yellow bus moves right past our house I get just a twinge of nostalgia for the past...and then I take another sip of coffee and I am over it!

I do remember our "last first" for our boys - the *last first* day of school. Beginning with Kindergarten each son had faithfully trudged for thirteen years, beginning with a monumental first day of school. Each experienced at the starting of their senior year in High School a last first day of school. Most every year on their first day of school I would bake them homemade cinnamon rolls. It seems as though it has been a long time since I last fired an oven up to bake those cinnamon rolls.

Once you become a parent the seasons marked by school take on a heightened significance. I remember holding nervous little hands, walking with them to the kindergarten class and thinking to myself, "This school is too big for my small children." Now both of my sons seem too big for any school to contain their dreams and ambitions. The school bus no longer stops for them; in fact, we live in different cities. When they visit they do not bring a drawing to post on the refrigerator. There have been many "last firsts" along the way; I just did not always know it or recognize it.

This is the way of life. Things come and move and have their being and then are no more. Life cannot be frozen or halted. Children grow up; parents get old; employment changes; friends move and the seasons unfold. In fact, growing involves shedding things along the way. Did you know that every five years 100 percent of our atoms turn over and are replaced by new ones? That is basically saying every five years we have a whole new self with no original parts. It is the nature of life to keep on moving. One scientist framed it this way: "We are continually being recreated from dust and returning to dust…we are not things; instead we are processes" (*More Than Meets the Eye*, Richard A. Swenson, p.18).

How do you see God in your "last firsts"; those places in your life where you are saying goodbye? What do you think is awaiting you? How do you trust God in these places of transitions? These are big questions applied in the minute particulars of life. No one place, home, church, or family can ever be exactly the way it was. That is the definition of death. Rather we are always in a process of becoming.

That is why we need each other in community, because together we share a pilgrimage. Together we may confess faithfully: "Jesus Christ is the same yesterday and today and forever." (Hebrews 13:8) But together we can draw into the mystery: "…forgetting what lies behind and straining forward to what lies ahead…" (Philippians 3:13).

Indeed, like seasons of the year and our own bodies we are growing and becoming. In all of our first lasts and endings that give birth to beginnings, may our confessions be that of the ancients: "The steadfast love of the LORD never ceases, his mercies never come to an end; they are new every morning; great is your faithfulness." (3:22-23).

Peace for the World – And All Therein

Peace. What an elusive word. In this season of giving thanks it can be difficult to be grateful when you are not experiencing peace.

Peace. It is sometimes difficult to imagine it. In our own country, we carve out lines of conflict according to color: red states and blue; and black versus white. Those called "peace keepers" make headlines because of accusations of brutality and in my middle years I wonder how much progress have we really made in terms of race relations. Religious differences add, in an ironic twist, to the conflict, with expressions of zealotry and extremism, at the cost of respect and sharing community.

Peace. It can be hard to come by. Ask the child frightened by gunfire in Gaza. Look at the housewife weary with abuse. Consider the alcoholic just trying to hang on.

Peace. When Jesus was born the angels sang about peace (Luke 2:9). When Jesus grew up he preached about peace, saying "Blessed are the peacemakers, for they will be called children of God," (Matthew 5:9). When he was resurrected he appeared to the disciples and said, "Peace be with you," (John 20:19).

Peace. It is a lovely word and it is a lovely thought and deep within us all is the longing for peace; to be whole; to be complete.

Just imagine that things could be different; that you and I do not have to go on living divided against others or divided against ourselves.

Just imagine that when you are in the tension between peace and conflict God is present.

The Great Story in scripture is the reminder that no matter how unpeaceful things may be in this world or in your life, it does not negate the presence of God. The Psalmist sings gently to us that God is pervasively, frustratingly, mercifully present to us.

Where can I go from your Spirit?

God is present in our loftiest ambitions… *If I ascend to heaven…*

God is present when we have hit rock bottom… *If I make my bed in Sheol…You are there.* (Ps 139)

We can flee, we can run, we can hide, we can fight, we can despair, we can blame, we can flail and fail and yet God is there, wherever "there" might be.

We can assume that we or events are beyond redemption, but that still will not be enough, because God is there.

If I take the wings of the morning and settle at the farthest limits of the sea, even there your hand shall lead me, and your right hand shall hold me fast. If I say, "Surely the darkness shall cover me, and the light around me become night," even the darkness is not dark to you; the night is as bright as the day, for darkness is as light to you.

Only when we come to a place of acknowledging and knowing God's abiding and pervasive presence can we embrace peace; perfect and complete peace. Knowing the presence of God dwelling beside us in our confusion and doubt or our bitterness and rage does not take away the conflict. It gives company to the conflict.

Peace. Peace does not come with more striving. To strive is to negate peace before it ever gets started. Peace comes not with more striving. Peace comes in the accepting.

Angels sang about it to the shepherds who did not seek it out and did nothing to earn it. Still they sang, "Glory to God in the highest heaven, and on earth Peace…"

Peace was the word that Jesus gave the frightened disciples hiding behind locked doors. "Peace be with you."

Peace is what God imagines for you, wherever you are and whatever you have done or not done. Peace because God is with you no matter what.

Where can I go from your spirit?
Or where can I flee from your presence?
If I ascend to heaven, you are there;
if I make my bed in Sheol, you are there.
If I take the wings of the morning and settle at the farthest limits of the sea,
even there your hand shall lead me,
and your right hand shall hold me fast.
(Psalm 139:6-10)

Life and Death are Not So Far Apart

Some years back I had the opportunity to travel to Kathmandu, Nepal to explore some of the mission work going on that country through an ecumenical partnership our church supported. Kathmandu is a wild, exotic city and every turn offered to me something new to see and experience.

One place I wanted to visit was Pashupatinath; a Hindu Temple where cremations occur all day, every day. I've always had a morbid curiosity about such things. I wish I could say it is because I have a high-minded, philosophical bent of pondering my own mortality. More to the truth, however, is I am just curious about many things, death being one of them.

Late one afternoon I made my way to the ancient temple grounds. The air was choked with the dust of human cremains, filling my hair, my eyes, and my ears with ashy remains. There were distant, piercing wails coming from grieving family members, mourning their dead loved ones. Soon I saw the pyres of wood lined up, many engulfed in flames, alongside the Baghmati River. As I squinted through the hazy dust I could clearly see limbs of corpses stacked upon the smoldering piles of wood. Periodically brooms routinely swept the charred cremains and coals of wood into the river, where family members bathed in oblation and prayer.

Ah death. For young and old; Hindu, Christian, Muslim or Jew; death comes to us all.

Annually Christians observe Ash Wednesday, the day in which we are called upon to reflect upon death. Many will attend services and will be marked by ashes in the sign of a cross, while hearing the words "from dust you come and to dust you shall return."

As a minister, I have led many of these services and can tell you first hand that it is a ponderous thing to impose these ashes upon the foreheads of friends, family, and strangers. I've marked the faces of the elderly, wondering would I see them for next years' service. Marking the children can be particularly sobering when they look up with earnestness, some even smiling kindly, innocently, as they say, "thank you," while I say, "…to dust you shall return."

Ash Wednesday is also a call for Christians to repent; to change directions. It is not just a time to reflect on ones' mortality, but to choose a different way to live. While remembering death, it is a day to also choose life as followers of the One who taught us to love abundantly.

Each year as I enter into the Lenten season of 40 days I mull over what it is I wish to give up; what will be my fast, as the tradition holds. Ultimately, I am choosing to fast from my language of death and change direction towards what is life-affirming. This means I will need to reject the language of anxiety and brutality that marks our political discourse and selfish ambitions. I will need to choose my words carefully, hold my offenses lightly, and walk circumspectly with deference to others. Only in letting go, Jesus reminds us, can we ever hope to gain.

In this journey where we are marked for death, I'm going to reflect not just on my own mortality, but this very life God has trusted me with to live fully, compassionately, mercifully, and generously with love for all. I am dust, and to dust I shall return. Therefore, today and all my remaining days I must love, because in the end that is all that will remain.

Everything else will be swept aside.

For Everything There is a Season

The afternoon was mild and warmed with welcome fall sunshine. Ten consecutive days of rain had created a muddy mess all around the barn, but none of us gathered there minded the mud so much. I was standing with my two brothers and father on a concrete slab layered in mud and manure, gently pushing Holsteins, Brown Swisses and Jerseys toward the barn for a final milking. After 103 years – over 75,000 consecutive milkings – the DeLoach & Sons Dairy was about to milk its last cow. Even though at the age of 18 I could not leave the farm fast enough, I was not going to miss it. Amy, Clark, a couple of nephews, my sister, and the wives of my daddy and brothers were not going to miss it either.

A switch was thrown and the familiar hum of the compressor that runs the milking machines came to life. It was time to milk the last herd of dairy cows. Outside four cattle trailers waited to load the cows and take them to the auction barn once the milking was complete. A local farmer who just a few years ago sold his herd came by to visit and commiserate. All of us laughed a bit, reminisced, and worked with cows placing the milking machines on their udders, and listening to the cows snort and blow, oblivious to their next move. A few brief hours later, as the sun began to cast its setting glow along the pastures out back, the last of the cows came through. Daddy milked the last one and just like that it was done. Once the barn was cleaned and put to order, he flipped the switched shutting everything down. Stepping out into dark evening, we watched the remaining truck leave transporting the cows destined for another pasture, another dairy.

The author of Ecclesiastes writes: "For everything there is a season, and a time for every matter under heaven…" (Ecclesiastes 3:1).

It is true with dairy barns, cows and people. Life is always turning and changing. Sometimes for the better and sometimes not, but life is always in motion. The only way we can experience the gifts of the future is to accept the changing from the old. It is also trusting the One who holds all seasons of time.

My daddy and brother will be fine. No doubt there will be a long period of adjustment from not having to get up very early in the morning for the first of two daily milkings, but they will be fine. A new season awaits, and with it are promises of generative beginnings.

So, it is for all of us in the passing of seasons. With every ending God has for us new beginnings. *The steadfast love of the LORD never ceases, his mercies never come to an end; they are new every morning; great is your faithfulness* (Lamentations 3:22-23).

This is the word of the Lord. It is true and can be trusted.

Faded Pictures and Faded Memories

For some time now Amy and I have been toying with the idea camping in Yellowstone National Park. We have camped there before, but it was a few years ago. Actually, it was many years ago. We were newlyweds about to move from garage apartment in Rome, GA to seminary housing in Louisville, KY. As we were boxing up our few belongings we determined we would have one great adventure before seminary, churches and children make the impracticality of such an adventure immutable. That was twenty-five years ago.

Here are a few things I remember: we drove for three days in a small car with nothing but a road atlas. Today that sounds simply foolish since we are pampered by GPS, smart phones and the internet guiding our every move. I remember that Yellowstone was cold; freezing actually. We prepared to camp as if we were setting up a tent in the Smoky Mountains of North Carolina in June. June in Wyoming is something altogether different. Each morning we awoke with the inside of our pup-tent glazed in ice, formed from our breathing during the night. I remember that the mountains were bigger than anything I had ever seen in my life, and yes, those mountains were covered in snow. I remember waiting for a long, long time to watch Old Faithful erupt (note: Old Faithful is not as faithful as it used to be). I remember taking a short hike to see the Grand Canyon of Yellowstone. I also remember seeing the remains of the great wildfire from the previous year (that was in 1988) and felt strangely sad by this act of nature.

Like I said, that was more than a few years ago. We decided to help our fading memories by looking at our pictures from that trip. The trouble is they were faded too! First, there were not that many pictures. I have always been a stingy photographer, especially during the era of film. Film cost money and developing and processing film cost money. There are few things more discouraging than getting your pictures from the developer only to discover most of them are either blurry or have a thumb over the lens. But I digress…The pictures that we did have were scant, faded, and did not tell much of the story. As much as I journal I cannot believe the only thing I have from that trip are faded pictures and faded memories.

Yet we *were* there and what we *remember* is that it was a special place at a special time in our lives. I suppose that is all that matters. Do you have stories that hold power and sway over your memories? Some stories give us joy and hope. And of course, some stories bring back pain and regret. With or without pictures we can never really go back and re-inhabit or relive the memory. It is in the past, yet it still has the power to shape and influence, whether our memories can be trusted or not.

The story that is most important is the one you are living today, right now. You have been shaped and are being shaped for this very moment to live, love, and be in community with others. There may be pictures, but most of the time there will be none. It is just now.

Practicing presence is not fretting over the failures or joys of the past and neither is it the anxious hoping for something better in the future. It is being present to others, particularly those whom you love. How many times have we looked back and remembered those who are now no longer in our lives and wished we had just one more memory, one more moment? The only moment is now.

Practicing presence is also a holy act of devotion. Too much of our religious vocabulary is paralyzed in a fixed dogma that imprisons our hopes for a better tomorrow while we anxiously try to figure it all out, reconstructing our past like a shattered piece of pottery. But God's eternity is now. Richard Rohr writes: "At this point, God becomes more a verb than a noun, more a process than a conclusion, more an experience than a dogma, more a personal relationship than an idea. There is Someone dancing with you…"

The truth is - at times the disquieting truth - is that memories and pictures *do* fade, for time will have its way every time. You and I are here, now. It is grace enough to name someone that you love, now. And grace enough to know that God is eternally moving in all of our "nows."

The most beautiful thing we can experience is the mysterious. It is the source of all true art and all science. He to whom this "emotion" is a stranger, who can no longer pause to wonder, or stand rapt in awe, is as good as dead. His eyes are closed.

- Albert Einstein

Peace for now, which is God's grace…

Before I Die…

I was in between appointments in an old section of Knoxville and decided to take advantage of my thirty minutes of downtime by wandering around the city. Deep down I felt certain I would eventually stumble across a good coffee shop, bakery, or maybe both! Turning a corner, I was initially disappointed to discover yet another scruffy alley, littered with the usual urban detritus. Along one of the walls of the alley, however, was a painting of sorts – a splash of graffiti from a reflective artist with a philosophic bent. In large letters three words were carefully painted: "Before I Die." Beneath the caption, lines were drawn in neat rows and columns, encouraging pedestrians to pause long enough to ponder and fill in the blanks with their respective answers. One person wrote, "Date your mom." Another scrawled, "Dance in the rain." A beleaguered fan wrote, "Titans make the playoffs," and a parent wished to "take my kids to the beach." Jimmy Buffett's name appeared several times, sometimes inappropriately. The one word I saw over and over again was "love."

One of the few things that separate us from the rest of the animal kingdom is that we have a knowledge that we will die. Daniel Ogilvie, a psychology professor at Rutgers, was giving a TED Talk about death and the soul. He tells the story of his four-year-old daughter. Late at night she had been lying in bed thinking and bolted upright, jumped out of bed, and raced into his bedroom crying saying, "I don't want to be a thing that dies!"

The thought of death, in spite of being surrounded in a culture of death, is terrifying for most us, and a topic usually avoided. Yet, knowing that one day our time will come can give us better focus on how we will live today. This is not about creating a "bucket list" or "seizing the day," but recognizing that life is too precious and valuable to waste. Henry David Thoreau acknowledged as much when he wrote: "As if you can kill time without injuring eternity."

The Psalmist writes: LORD, *let me know my end, and what is the measure of my days; let me know how fleeting my life is* (39:4); and *teach us to count our days that we may gain a wise heart* (90:12). We want to know such things because it intensifies how precious this life is. It grounds us in a sense of urgency – not frantic hopelessness.

When we understand, albeit haltingly, that life is fleeting, we can then *die* to those things that do not count or matter and will not live on. It opens us up, as with the baptism covenant in Paul's letter to the Romans, to the life God has created for us to live in.

"We have been buried with him by baptism into death..." Death is not something to be denied. Death is not something to be ignored. Death is not something to entertain. Death is not something to be treated carelessly. Death is the teacher of life. And when we die in the mystical union of Christ, we are then set free to be raised up to *"walk in newness of life..."* (Romans 6)

There is too much emphasis, I think, on eternal life as after life. Certainly, in the teachings of Jesus it is clear he believed in life after death. But it is also clear that eternal life begins now. The problem with seeing eternal life as only about the afterlife is that it focuses our attention on the next world *instead of transformation in this world.* "I have come," says the Teacher, "that you might have life, and have it in abundance."

Before I die...Love. Let us then place love not on a list of things to be accomplished before we die, but in our living, day by day, moment by moment. Love is all that remains when our breath becomes air and God receives us back as eternity rolls on and on and on...

Blood Moon

It was not only the month of the Blood Moon, on that particular morning it was a lunar eclipse. The moon in all of its full glory was glowing an eerie shade of red affected by the earth's shadow. I read that the best place to view the eclipse was in the middle of the Pacific Ocean. I believe my side of the hemisphere proved to be a lovely spot too. I first noticed it that morning when I was out jogging, which is often a lovely time to watch the stars when not watching where I am going.

While we admire the Blood Moon and this rare eclipse, the ancients often viewed such celestial events with a foreboding sense of dread and fear. Not knowing what they were seeing, it was assumed that it was a portent of things to come. Now we know better and even can predict the next one. A few hundred years ago it was thought that the earth was the center of the universe. Now we know that not only is the earth not the center of the universe, but it is not even the center of the solar system of this galaxy. Furthermore, our galaxy, according to some astronomers, is just one of hundreds of billions of galaxies. Our solar system is more like a suburb among the other galaxies, known and unknown.

The very thought alone draws me into a sense of Biblical awe and reverence. Long before telescopes the Psalmist thought as much. In Psalm 8 David wrote (and no doubt sung) "When I look at your heavens, the work of your fingers, the moon and the stars that you have established; what are human beings that you are mindful of them, mortals that you care for them?" Again, in Psalm 19 we read: "The heavens are telling the glory of God; and the firmament proclaims his handiwork. Day to day pours forth speech, and night to night declares knowledge."

As much as we now know about the heavens and the spheres, there is so much we do not know. Ralph Waldo Emerson wrote: "Knowledge is knowing that we cannot know." This is not an excuse for ignorance mind you; just a humble reminder that life is vast and ultimately incomprehensible. We do not know about the future, much less our present. We do not know about how it will all work out with our families, our finances, our health or even our church. There is only so much telescopes and microscopes can tell us. The rest is mystery…holy, sacred mystery.

It is not what we know that validates our faith. It is Who we know that graces us with peace. Both knowledge and ignorance can shackle us to fear and its sibling anxiety. To rest in the "Name above all names" can set us free.

To the one struggling to find a job…*may the peace of Christ hold you.*

To the one whose family is a disaster…*may the presence of God sustain you.*

To the one cowed by the "dark cloud" of anxiety…*may the comfort of the Spirit fill you.*

To all of us propelled forward in this expanding universe headed into an uncertain future, *may we look up and experience the Word that calls forth creation to live, to love, and to hope.*

All of Life Summed Up in a Cashew Can

Since at least the 10th century, Christians around the world mark the beginning of the Lenten journey with Ash Wednesday. For observant churches, the young and old are invited to come forward to be marked with a cross of ashes, customarily on the forehead. At the point of marking, the minister or priest will repeat the words, "...you are dust, and to dust you shall return." (Genesis 3:19)

The first year I hosted an Ash Wednesday service, I solicited the help from a neighboring church far more experienced in the observance of Ash Wednesday. The thoughtful chair of the altar guild offered to give me a can of ashes, saving me the trouble of burning, sifting and mixing the ash mixture. On the appointed day, she had the prepared ashes waiting for me to pick up at their church.

When I arrived to collect the ashes, she had placed them in a simple can (formally cashews, which I am sure was a surprise for anybody reaching in for a few nuts). On the lid of the can she had scrawled in magic marker the following words: *Ashes – Greg DeLoach (he is not in here).* This is an important disclaimer that I am happy to confirm.

Yet is this not what Ash Wednesday is about - a time to reflect on our own mortality as well as repentance? Philosophers have long claimed that the way to prepare for life is to contemplate death. Morbid? I don't think so. Often Jesus spoke of the need to release one's life (which is in itself an enormous act of faith) in order to gain it (Matthew 10:7; 16:25). Furthermore, Ash Wednesday marks the beginning of Jesus' journey to the deadly timbers of the cross.

We are surrounded by silly symbols of our anxieties that oftentimes are manifested in over-consumption and violence. Yet we are all, in the end, destined to be no more than a can of ashes on this earth. Ash Wednesday and Lent call on us to ignore the anxious voices that cannot believe in anything but the self, and listen to the voice of the One who, out of dust, breathed in each the breath of life. There will come a day when our breath returns to the Creator.

Finally, the ashes that mark us on Ash Wednesday are an invitation to follow. For me this season is an important reminder that whatever it is I face or will face in my life – and one can scarcely imagine what awaits us in our lifetime – its scope does not exceed the reach of God. I do not know how I will face all that confronts me, but then again that is not my primary concern. I am called to follow on this journey.

Losing in Order to Gain

I had just wrapped up a 14-mile trek that began near the top of Newfound Gap and descended to Deep Creek in the Great Smoky Mountain National Park. Although the trail was largely one of descents, it was a slog in places that involved stomping through muddy bogs, wading across streams, and pushing through bramble so thick that at times I could not even see the trail beneath my feet. By the time I arrived at Deep Creek I was sweaty and speckled in black mud, and was tattooed with a few welts from horse-fly bites.

It would be another hour before Amy would arrive to pick me up, so I took advantage of the cold stream and bathed off the grime, leaving my boots, shirt, hiking stick and daypack beside an old birch tree. Right on time, an hour later Amy pulls up and, throwing my gear in the back of the jeep, we left the trail for the campsite.

It wasn't until the next day that I realized I had left my walking stick behind.

I have had this walking stick for about 15 or so years. Clark, my oldest son, made it for me from a dogwood sapling. It is light and solid, and has been my hiking companion through the years and along the trails. It has dutifully kept its place during a snowstorm, propped outside my tent like a sentinel keeping watch. It has scared away copperheads that were near my thudding steps. This walking stick has durably held up to all the grime that comes along with any hike.

When I discovered that my walking stick did not make it back to camp, we circled back to the trailhead to look for it. It was raining and quite frankly I had pretty much given it up as lost. I thought, "who would pass up a perfectly good staff, abandoned beside a tree?"

With an umbrella in hand, a traipsed alongside the swollen creek looking for the spot where I bathed the evening before. I had little expectation that I would see it again, and I was already telling myself that it was going to be okay. Buddhists teach about the importance of 'non-attachment,' and Jesus reminds us to not lay up treasures here on earth." Just as I was about to head back to the Jeep in the steady rain, with my head hanging low, I spotted it. My walking stick was just as I left it, propped against the birch tree and waiting, it seemed to me, for the next hike.

I felt a bit foolish feeling so emotional about a stick. I am sentimental about things, especially those objects associated with my children, but this seemed a bit different.

In psychoanalytical terminology, my walking stick could be described as a "transition object" – something to provide psychological comfort. I guess that walking stick is true enough for me.

Growing older I am learning to walk lighter. I am not simply referring to "stuff" that clutters my home and office; artifacts I have accumulated along the way and kept (hoarded?) sentimentally. By walking lighter, I am coming to recognize that it is okay that not everything has to be significant or have a purpose (including me) or lasting value. I have a place and a part to play in this moment and that is all that is necessary for the time.

If you travel long enough, you will lose stuff as you go, and that is okay.

A friend introduced to me a poem after I told him the story of the walking stick. It is a poem I return to often. It is by the Polish poet Czeslaw Melos.

Love
Love means to learn to look at yourself
The way one looks at distant things
For you are only one thing among many.
And whoever sees that way heals his heart,
Without knowing it, from various ills.
A bird and a tree say to him: Friend.

Then he wants to use himself and things

So that they stand in the glow of ripeness.
It doesn't matter whether he knows what he serves:
Who serves best doesn't always understand.

"You are only one among many." The older I get the more I know that this is truth. This is not a sigh of quiet resignation, but a relief that I really am not the center of the universe. I will walk this good earth for a time, but in time no more.

The next line is particularly poignant for me: "Then he wants to use himself and things / So that they stand in the glow of ripeness." Richard Rohr has written about the importance of the second half of life in his book "Falling Upward." In it he reflects: "When you get your, 'Who am I?', question right, all of your, 'What should I do?' questions tend to take care of themselves"

I am walking these days with less frantic purpose, but more meaning; less urgency, but more sincerity; less fear, yet more openness to wonder.

I will hang on to my walking stick for a while yet. As Robert Frost once penned, there are "miles to go before I sleep." There will come a day, of course, in which I need to just let it go. And that will be okay too.

"It doesn't matter whether he knows what he serves:
Who serves best doesn't always understand."

A Wandering Life

One fall morning, when I was a little boy of eight years old, I took it upon myself to leave the house and explore the vast pastures and woods of our farm. In the past, my daddy and granddaddy walked every acre with me, but this was the first time I struck out on my own and by myself – and without the consent or knowledge of anyone else! I traipsed directly to the creek that dissected our land, found a narrow pass and jumped over to the other side. I figured that soon I should be climbing a familiar hill that would overlook the pastures with the dairy cows grazing on one side and the creek bottoms on the other. Instead I came to another creek – this was a surprise – and it seemed to me it was on the wrong side. Then and there it slowly occurred to me that I was not exactly lost, but rather confused. I had walked in a circle.

For the last century researchers have puzzled over why when we walk we generally do not travel in a straight line, especially without a fixed point. This is also true for swimming and driving a car. Without a fixed point, we tend to travel in circles. Scientists and engineers can put a man on the moon, but there is still not a good answer as to why we travel in circles, even when we think we are going straight ahead. By the way, I do not recommend you drive a car blindfolded to test this theory out, but I am told it is true.

In this life, we wander. We make plans, draw up maps, put forth sincere intentions, but as we journey along we inevitably take twists and turns and sometimes move in circles. A disappointment here, a surprise there, an interruption along the way, and before we know it we find that we are just wandering around.

Has your life turned out exactly like you planned it or thought it would go? Of course not. In this life, we wander. No matter how much we plan, prepare, and pray, life is not a straight line, a sure path, or a fixed way. Physicists speak of the Theory of Indeterminacy (or chaos theory). Theologians just call it life. We are all living it and if you feel as though sometimes you are going in circles you are not alone.

This is the story of God's treasured people called Israel. It describes their life in the wilderness. Not only for forty years did they wander around, but for all its history they have wandered. The author of Hebrews describes the faithful of Israel as "…strangers and foreigners on the earth." (11:13) It is as if they were born and exist to wander.

We are a wandering people too. The *Missio Dei* – the mission of God – is not about following a plan to prevent the wandering. Rather it is to embrace this wandering life, wherever it takes us with all its surprises, disappointments and interruptions, and to do so trusting in the presence and provision of God, who has wandered into our way.

My hope for the church is that we grow more and more intentional in meeting people where they are in their wandering. This means allowing space for their questions and room for their searching. This is not about unqualified relativism, but a trust that when we seek, God may be found. "When you search for me, you will find me; if you seek me with all your heart." (Jeremiah 29.13).

Peace be with you…

A Generous Stack of Wood

> *"Every man looks upon his wood pile with a sort of affection."*
> - Henry David Thoreau

All of my life I have enjoyed the blessings of the generosity of others. This includes procuring firewood. I have friends in the church that have allowed me to cut wood, gather wood, and at times some have delivered wood practically to my doorstep. Few things in housekeeping are more satisfying than a generous stack of firewood. Thoreau continued his soliloquy on firewood writing, "*I love to have mine before my window, and the more chips the better to remind me of my pleasing work.*"

Yet no matter how grand the stack, as winter's chill sets in so goes the wood. Firewood was meant to burn to warm both home and heart. The cycle of generosity repeats itself: find, cut, split and deliver more wood year in and year out.

We spend our days accumulating and then in time we begin giving it all away. I have been reminded of this lesson of late as I know of several in our church family who are "downsizing" from larger homes to smaller ones. There is the sentimental and at times painful sorting through a lifetime of artifacts trying to determine what to keep, what to give away and what to throw out. Meanwhile the concentric circles of life grow smaller and smaller. Such is life.

It is at this liminal and sacred place that grants us space to reflect on what it is in this world that is most valuable and what it is that we will take with us even into the grave. I collect and horde, cherish and sentimentalize so many things and so much stuff. But in truth, like my seasonally diminishing woodpile, it will in the end come to nothing. There are a few things, however, that are worth my whole life.

Jesus once mused, "What does it profit them if they gain the whole world, but lose or forfeit themselves?" (Luke 9:25) When my time is done, I hope that my woodpile has been used up. I hope that the love for my wife and children will be complete with nothing held back. I hope that when the earth claims the last of my remains all of me will have been given completely away.

Let us love one another generously. Let us celebrate what we have and not what we wish we had. Let us in due time give it all away so that those who come behind us may be warmed by our fires.

You Are Not Your Own

I grew up with a family where church was simply a part of life together. It was, and still is, a small church embedded in a rural county, surrounded by thickets of pines and pastures of hay. A portrait of Jesus hanging on the wall stared at me every Sunday as we recited the Apostle's Creed. From the little, brown and slightly tattered Cokesbury hymnal our mighty congregation of about 30 would sing "Dwelling in Beulah Land," although no one in particular was in a hurry to go there any time soon.

Since my beginning, and I am certain at my *very* beginning, it was impressed upon me that my life was not my own and that I am a part of something much bigger than my solitary life. I stopped being the center of my universe many years ago, although my own orbit still tugs against the hidden gravity keeping me from being fully consumed with self-centeredness.

I suppose you are expecting me to write about all the certainties I have unearthed along the way about faith. I will save those sermons for other pulpits. I am content enough to saunter deeper into mystery. It is enough for me to know that I am but a part of the Great Mystery's work.

My mentor, Thomas Merton, who died two years after I was born, wrote:

…if we could let go of our own obsession with what we think is the meaning of it all, we might be able to hear His call and follow Him in His mysterious, cosmic dance.

I have spent the better part of my first few decades trying to wrestle out meaning and purpose behind every act and every event. Now I am okay with simply peace. Purpose has its place, but purpose, at the risk of redundancy, is not the purpose.

My life, according to the Apostle Paul, is not my own (1 Corinthians 6:19). It is not about me, and I am okay with that. When I hear a lonely Whippoorwill on a hot summer evening; when the air is thick with the smell of smoke from a campfire; when the noise of a crashing surf lulls me to a sweet emptying; or when I look up and the stars shimmer and pulse with the life of the universe, I am at peace that my life is not my own. I am not the center, but I am a part and have a place, and that is blessed peace.

...no despair of ours can alter the reality of things; or stain the joy of the cosmic dance which is always there. Indeed, we are in the midst of it, and it is in the midst of us, for it beats in our very blood, whether we want it to or not.
Yet the fact remains that we are invited to forget ourselves on purpose, cast our awful solemnity to the winds and join in the general dance. (Thomas Merton, New Seeds of Contemplation)

The Grace of Doing Nothing

I am not very good at doing "nothing." I am easily distracted; fidgety; and deep down carry the deceptive belief that I should always be "productive." Productivity is a lie we tell ourselves so that we may feel valuable. Nevertheless, I struggle with this lie and have spent too much of my life shouldering this onerous burden with busyness. Family vacations have taught me a different path; a path of passive resistance.

I did not grow up with a family that took regular vacations. It was a luxury of time we did not have on a dairy farm that operates with milkings twice a day, every day. I can remember going on four distinct vacations with members of my family. When I was 8 years old we took a vacation to Disney World. The park had just opened a couple of years earlier and it is still one of my favorite childhood memories. A few years later my grandparents took us to the Smoky Mountains for a few days. Those mountains still have a hold on me. The first time I remember seeing the ocean was on a quick trip to Daytona Beach. Another time I went to Destin Beach with my maternal grandparents. The ocean holds its own kind of mystery and I never tire in hearing the tide come in.

These four vacations all occurred within the first twelve years of my life, and I am grateful for each one. After that, if we wanted to see the mountains or go to the beach we had to find a way on our own. Time was a luxury that just did not allow for those kinds of family outings. We did have the luxury of family, and that is a gift that cannot be reduced to a photograph or postcard or souvenir.

Every year of our marriage we have enjoyed both the luxury of time and family to appreciate a vacation. The term vacation literally means to vacate or take freedom from something. Vacations are a break in routine; a change in the monotony of expectations. Vacations are also a time of rest; a season to simply "be." They give us the privilege of, as Richard Niebuhr phrases it, "the grace of doing nothing."

Although as a child our family rarely went anywhere beyond the county line, we all knew the luxury of slowing down and resting.

Some of my favorite memories in the summer included sitting in lawn chairs in the front yard and talking about nothing while the cows sauntered nearby chewing their cud. It was pleasure enough to rest, to hear stories, and to share dreams and hopes for the future.

I go among trees and sit still.
All my stirring becomes quiet
Around me like circles on water.
My tasks lie in their places
Where I left them, asleep like cattle
(Wendell Berry, Sabbaths)

Well I am grown up now, mostly. Every year I question the expense of our vacation and wonder if I can afford it, but deep down I know – there will be enough, and I cannot afford not to go.

My friends and family, with whom I vacation with each year, have served as valuable teachers on the grace of doing nothing. For a brief window of time we sit along the coast on grainy beach chairs and rest, hear stories and share dreams and hopes for the future.

Now that I am in my 50s I am learning that this is a grace that should not be squandered.

"Stand at the crossroads, and look, and ask for the ancient paths, where the good way lies; and walk in it, and find rest for your souls." (Jeremiah 6:16)

www.ingramcontent.com/pod-product-compliance
Lightning Source LLC
Chambersburg PA
CBHW052133110526
44591CB00012B/1703